D0038182

Heaven for Kids

Tyndale House Publishers
Carol Stream, Illinois

HEAVEN for Kids

RANDY ALCORN

WITH LINDA WASHINGTON

Visit Randy Alcorn's website at epm.org.

TYNDALE and Tyndale's quill logo are registered trademarks of Tyndale House Publishers.

The Lion, the Witch and the Wardrobe and *Narnia* are trademarks of C. S. Lewis (Pte) Ltd.

Heaven for Kids

Copyright © 2006 by Eternal Perspective Ministries. All rights reserved.

Cover photograph © by Andersen Ross/Getty Images. All rights reserved.

Handwriting copyright © 2006 by Adrianna Nuñez. All rights reserved.

Designed by Jacqueline L. Nuñez

Edited by Betty Free Swanberg

Unless otherwise indicated, all Scripture quotations are taken from the *Holy Bible,* New Living Translation, copyright © 1996, 2004 by Tyndale House Foundation. Used by permission of Tyndale House Publishers, Carol Stream, Illinois 60188. All rights reserved.

Scripture quotations marked NIV are taken from the Holy Bible, *New International Version,*® *NIV.*® Copyright © 1973, 1978, 1984 by Biblica, Inc.® Used by permission. All rights reserved worldwide.

Scripture quotations marked NKJV are taken from the New King James Version®. Copyright © 1982 by Thomas Nelson. Used by permission. All rights reserved.

Scripture quotations marked ESV are from The ESV® Bible (The Holy Bible, English Standard Version®), copyright © 2001 by Crossway, a publishing ministry of Good News Publishers. Used by permission. All rights reserved.

Scripture quotations marked NASB are taken from the New American Standard Bible,® copyright © 1960, 1962, 1963, 1968, 1971, 1972, 1973, 1975, 1977, 1995 by The Lockman Foundation. Used by permission.

For manufacturing information regarding this product, please call 1-800-323-9400.

For information about special discounts for bulk purchases, please contact Tyndale House Publishers at csresponse@tyndale.com, or call 1-800-323-9400.

Library of Congress Cataloging-in-Publication Data

Alcorn, Randy C.
   Heaven for kids / Randy Alcorn ; based on Randy Alcorn's book Heaven ; adapted for kids by Randy Alcorn ; with Linda Washington.
   p. cm.
   ISBN 978-1-4143-1040-4 (sc : alk. paper)
   1. Heaven—Christianity—Juvenile literature.   I. Washington, Linda M.
II. Title.
   BT846.3.A433 2006
   236′.24—dc22   2006011261

Printed in China

29   28   27   26   25   24   23
20   19   18   17   16   15   14

To Alexis Greenley, Spencer Greenley,
Mckinzie Bowles, Zachary Bowles,
and
Logan Noren,
the precious children of our nieces and nephews
Joe and Chris Greenley,
Grant and Denise Bowles,
and
Brad and LaVon Noren

Contents

Chapter Four:

What Is the New Earth? What Will

Chapter Five:

Who Rules?..75

Acknowledgments

I want to thank the following people for their significant contributions to this book:

Linda Washington, for taking my book Heaven, *selecting the parts that seemed most suitable for kids, and jazzing them up. This gave me a big head start in undertaking my revisions.*

Betty Swanberg, for her skilled, thoughtful, and helpful editing, and for being so easy to work with.

Karen Watson and Jan Axford, for also being a pleasure to work with, and for doing their jobs at Tyndale House so well.

Elizabeth Gosnell, for her diligence in the unsung labors of copyediting.

Tiffany Pate, Amy Campbell, and Angie Obrist, for looking this over in its early form and offering the invaluable perspectives of moms involved in their children's educations.

Doreen Button and Tim Newcomb, for reading through every line and suggesting further revisions.

Bonnie Hiestand, for tirelessly typing in many of my changes.

Kathy Norquist, for helping clean up the manuscript before submission.

Sarah Ballenger, for researching several important items for me.

Linda Jeffries and Janet Albers, for their great work at EPM, which frees me to write books.

Nanci, my awesome wife, who brings such joy and encouragement to every aspect of my life.

Jesus, the One whom Heaven and the New Earth will be all about. It will be so wonderful, Lord, precisely because you are so wonderful. Thank you for offering Heaven to people like me . . . and every kid and adult who reads this book!

Note to the Reader

How many times have you thought about Heaven in the last week? Have you brought up the subject or asked anyone a question about Heaven? Unless a person or a pet close to you has died (or is dying), the topic of Heaven may not have crossed your mind. Still, since you have this book in your hand, you're already *beginning* to think about Heaven. Good for you!

This book has questions many people have asked about life after death. As you read it, you might find some of the questions *you've* asked. You'll probably also find some questions you've never *thought* about asking. But I think you'll find most of them very interesting. I've tried to base my answers to these questions on what God tells us about Heaven in the Bible. (There are a lot of wrong ideas about Heaven, but we can always depend on what the Bible has to say.) At the beginning of each chapter, you'll find two quotes—one from the Bible and one from The Chronicles of Narnia— that will start you thinking about the ideas in the chapter.

But now it's time to turn the page and take a look at the first question and answer. You may want to read just one at a time, or you may read several in one sitting. You'll probably want to look up some of the Bible verses too. You and your family could do that together. It's always fun to talk with your friends about the things you're reading, so you could bring up what you're learning with them.

Enjoy exploring life in Heaven. After all, it's a place where *you* can live forever someday—a place without fear, anger, sadness, or sickness. And it's not just a place without bad stuff. It's a place full of *great* stuff: beauty, joy, fun, lots of activity, and rest when you need it. We'll have endless adventures together with Jesus and each other. It's a place where you can live with the wonderful and fascinating God who created you. And it's a place where you can hang out with all sorts of kind and interesting people who will be your friends forever.

Cool!

Anyway, I really hope you enjoy this book!

Randy Alcorn

Introduction

We are citizens of heaven, where the Lord Jesus Christ lives. And we are eagerly waiting for him to return as our Savior.

PHILIPPIANS 3:20

[Jewel the Unicorn] cried: "I have come home at last! This is my real country! I belong here. This is the land I have been looking for all my life, though I never knew it till now. The reason why we loved the old Narnia is that it sometimes looked a little like this. . . . Come further up, come further in!"

C. S. LEWIS, *The Last Battle*

Do I really need to think about Heaven?

Suppose your dad or mom told you that you were moving to a new place. What's the first thing you'd do? Ask questions, right? You'd want to know the *who, what, when, where,* and *why* about the place where you were going to live.

Now pretend you're part of a NASA team preparing for a five-year mission to Mars. After a period of heavy-duty training, the launch date finally arrives. As the rocket lifts off, one of the other astronauts says to you, "What do you know about Mars?"

Imagine shrugging your shoulders and saying, "Nothing. We never talked about it. I guess we'll find out when we get there." Think that would happen? Not likely, right? Part of your training would have prepared you for where you would be living for the next five years. You would have talked about Mars 24/7, wouldn't you? *After all, that's where you were headed!*

Maybe at some point you've said, "I believe Jesus died for the wrong things I've done" (more about that in chapter ten). Perhaps you've already asked for his forgiveness and placed your trust in him. If so, the Bible promises that Heaven will be your future home. Jesus said so himself. "There is more than enough room in my Father's home. If this were not so, would I have told you that I am going to prepare a place for you? When everything is ready, I will come and get you, so that you will always be with me where I am" (John 14:2-3).

When my family goes on a trip, we like to know in advance what it's like where we're going. If we're planning a vacation, we look at the brochures and maps and Web sites. We learn about the attractions—all the things that make it a place we want to visit.

Finding out in advance about the Grand Canyon or Disney World or summer camp helps us get excited and look forward to going there. The Bible says, "We are looking forward to the new heavens and new earth he has promised, a world filled with God's righteousness" (2 Peter 3:13). But we won't really look forward to that place unless we know something about its attractions before we get there, right?

So if Heaven—or as that verse calls it, "the new heavens and new earth"—will be your home someday, wouldn't it be great to learn all you can about it now? That way you can spend your whole life looking forward to the place that will be your home forever!

That's what this book is all about.

Isn't it enough just to think about being with Jesus?

Each of us is made for a person. And we're also made for a place. Jesus is the person. Heaven is the place.

Jesus lives in Heaven and is getting a place ready for us there. So if we look forward to being with Jesus, that's the same as looking forward to Heaven. Why? Because that's where we'll be with him. So whenever we think about being with Jesus, we're thinking about Heaven. And whenever we think about Heaven, we should be thinking about Jesus.

What do I look forward to?

Are you *really* looking forward to going to Heaven? Maybe in seventy or eighty years, right? After you've done all the things you want to do.

Think about some things you do look forward to:

- Christmas or another favorite holiday

- Your birthday, your sister's birthday (well, maybe not), or even your dog's birthday

- Going to your favorite place (like a water park, the beach, the woods, the river, or maybe SeaWorld or Six Flags)

- The last day of school and the start of summer vacation

- Seeing a movie you've been told is really, really good

- Getting the next book in your favorite series

Why do you look forward to those things? "Duh," you might say. The answer is obvious. Because of what you already know about these things, you use your God-given imagination. You can almost taste, feel, smell, hear, and see all of the wonderful things you expect.

For example, if your birthday's coming up, you might taste, feel, smell, hear, and see chocolate cake with thick frosting, the laughter of friends,

and presents. Maybe you're looking forward to
seeing cousins, aunts, and uncles you haven't seen
in a while. Or perhaps you're counting on getting
lots of cool presents.

But guess what? Looking forward to Heaven
is no different. In fact, looking forward to Heaven
is even better than looking forward to Christmas
or your birthday! Yet many people find that hard
to believe because they don't know how to picture
Heaven. They don't know how to look forward
to it.

Does that describe you?

What do people believe about Heaven?

Speaking of describing, what are some words you
would use to describe Heaven? Would *fun* and *exciting* be words you'd use?

It might surprise you to discover that many people find no joy at all when they think about Heaven.
Wondering why? They don't look forward to going
there because of what they believe Heaven is like.

Gary Larson showed a common view of
Heaven in one of his *Far Side* cartoons. In it a man
with angel wings and a halo sits on a cloud, doing
nothing, with no one nearby. He has the expression

of someone stuck on a desert island, bored because he has absolutely nothing to do. A caption shows what he's thinking: "Wish I'd brought a magazine."

Is that your view of what Heaven will be like? Or is it what someone you know thinks? Many people fear that Heaven will be . . . well, boring.

When you were younger, maybe you saw the movie *All Dogs Go to Heaven*. Think w-a-a-a-y back. Charles B. Barkin (Charlie), a German shepherd, goes to Heaven because, of course, everyone thinks "all dogs go to Heaven"! But Charlie doesn't want to be in Heaven. Why? Because there are no surprises—no exciting ones anyway. Everything is predictable. Even the temperature is a steady seventy-three degrees Fahrenheit, which sounds boring to Charlie. He prefers the excitement of life on Earth to an eternity of floating on a cloud, wearing wings and a halo. So he ditches Heaven to return to Earth.

In the sequel (*All Dogs Go to Heaven 2*), Charlie explains his frustrations with Heaven when he sings, "It's too heavenly here. It's too peaceful and paradise-like." In other words, Heaven is too dull for him.

Predictable? Boring? Endless years of the same old, same old? No one would look forward to that!

Well, I've got some good news for you. Charlie got it all wrong. Heaven is not like that at all. *No way!*

Have you ever read any of the books about Peter Pan and wished you could live in a beautiful, magical place like Neverland—but without Captain Hook and all the mean pirates? Well, Heaven is a better place than Neverland any day. How do I know? From what the Bible says about it.

That's why this book provides another view of Heaven: as a place worth thinking and talking and dreaming about. In fact, once you understand what the Bible really says about Heaven, *you can't help but look forward to living there!*

Chapter 1

WHAT CAN WE KNOW ABOUT HEAVEN?

He showed me the holy city, Jerusalem, descending out of heaven from God. It shone with the glory of God and sparkled like a precious stone. . . . The city wall was broad and high. . . . The twelve gates were made of pearls. . . . And the main street was pure gold, as clear as glass. . . . The glory of God illuminates the city, and the Lamb is its light. The nations will walk in its light.

REVELATION 21:10-12, 21, 23-24

*"I bet there isn't a country like this anywhere in our world. Look
at the colours! You couldn't get a blue like the blue on those moun-
tains in our world."*
"Is it not Aslan's country?" said Tirian. . . .
*"Those hills," said Lucy, "the nice woody ones and the blue ones
behind—aren't they very like the southern border of Narnia?"*
*"Like!" cried Edmund after a moment's silence. "Why, they're
exactly like. . . ."*
"And yet they're not like," said Lucy. . . . "They're more . . . more . . ."
"More like the real thing," said the Lord Digory softly.

C. S. Lewis, *The Last Battle*

Is Heaven a real place?

Before I answer that question, let me tell you a
story. Starting in AD 1271, an explorer named
Marco Polo traveled from his hometown of Venice, Italy, to China and didn't go home for twenty-
four years. Talk about a l-o-o-n-g trip! When he
returned to Venice, he described a world that the
people of Italy had never seen. Although China
was a real place, it was very different from Italy.
So Marco Polo had to use word pictures and ideas
that people in Venice knew in order to describe
what he saw.

In *The Travels of Marco Polo,* he described
the city now called Beijing by saying, "It is walled

around with walls of earth. . . . There are 12 gates, and over each gate there is a great and handsome palace. . . . All the plots of ground on which the houses of the city are built are four-square, and laid out with straight lines. . . . Each square plot is surrounded by handsome streets for the traffic. Thus the whole city is arranged in squares just like a chessboard."

Think about what you would do if you were trying to describe a place you've seen but no one else has. You would probably compare that place to other familiar places, saying, "It was like . . ." or, "It reminded me of . . ." That's what John, one of Jesus' twelve disciples, and other writers of the Bible did to help their readers understand what Heaven is like. They describe Heaven as a garden, a city, a country, a kingdom, and "paradise."

But many people still aren't sure that Heaven is a real place. They even believe people in Heaven are ghosts floating on clouds. The Bible tells us that Heaven *is* a real place—just as real as planet Earth. In fact, God calls the place we'll live forever the "New Earth."

We're human beings. We're not made to live as ghosts in a ghostly place—especially on clouds!

(No one can live on a cloud anyway. If you've flown in an airplane, you've seen clouds up close. They're made of water!)

If we know Jesus, we will enter Heaven when we die. And some time after Jesus comes back to Earth, God promises he will bring us to live on the New Earth—a world with ground, trees, and water: "Look! I am creating new heavens and a new earth, and no one will even think about the old ones anymore" (Isaiah 65:17).

This place will be beautiful beyond our wildest imagination. (But that doesn't mean we shouldn't use our imaginations when we think about it now!)

Where do we get our ideas about Heaven?

What would you call someone who lies to you, steals from you, and is mean to you all the time? You'd call that person an enemy. (No, this isn't a description of your cousin or the kid who keeps annoying you at school.)

As you may know, Christians have an enemy.

He goes by different names: Lucifer, Satan, and the devil.

In *The Lion, the Witch and the Wardrobe*, the White Witch is like the devil.

"She is a perfectly terrible person," said Lucy. "She calls herself the Queen of Narnia though she has no right to be queen at all. . . . And she can turn people into stone and do all kinds of horrible things. And she has made a magic so that it is always winter in Narnia—always winter, but it never gets to Christmas."

Maybe you like winter. I do. But not one that lasts a hundred years! That's how long it has been winter in Narnia because of the Witch's spell. Most creatures have never seen another season. I'd hate to have winter without Christmas, wouldn't you? That's the best part about winter. But Satan doesn't want us to believe in Jesus or think about him. Just like the White Witch doesn't want anyone to believe in Aslan or think about him.

(By the way, in some stories, like *The Wizard of Oz*, white witches are good. But in Narnia the *white* in "White Witch" represents the coldness and death of sin. In fact, there is no such thing as a good witch in Narnia . . . or in the Bible. Deuteronomy 18:10-14 is a warning against witchcraft, fortune-telling, sorcery, omens, mediums, psychics, and anyone attempting to talk to the dead. God wants you to stay away from those things, including Ouija boards and tarot cards, because he hates them. If friends try to talk you into these things, you need to tell them *no* and talk to your parents, and maybe even find other friends.)

The White Witch is always lying. If you've read the book or seen the movie, you'll remember how she lies to Edmund and makes him think she is going to be nice to him. And she tries to get him to betray his brother and sisters. The Witch lies about Aslan. In the same way, Satan lies to us about Jesus. And he lies about God's home—Heaven.

Jesus said of the devil, "When he lies, he speaks his native language, for he is a liar and the father of lies" (John 8:44, niv). Some of Satan's favorite lies are about Heaven. He doesn't want you to know what an awesome place it really is! He doesn't want you to love Jesus or go to Heaven or look forward to it.

The devil was thrown out of Heaven for trying to make himself equal with God (Isaiah 14:12-15). He became bitter, not only toward God, but also toward people and Heaven itself. He had tried to take over Heaven but was kicked out. Maybe this sounds like a made-up story, but it's true. The Bible says it really happened.

We're told this about the White Witch: "It was part of her magic that she could make things look like what they aren't." Satan is always doing that. He's always doing it about Heaven, and unfortunately it has worked. He has made Heaven look boring. Satan doesn't need to convince us that Heaven isn't real. He only needs to make us believe that Heaven is a place we wouldn't enjoy. It's like planning a trip to Disney World or some other fun place and being told by a kid who has been permanently banned from there (because he tried to set it on fire or something), "Oh, you'll hate it at Disney World. It's boring."

If we believe what Satan says about Heaven, we won't want to live there or even think about it. But since we know that Satan is really good at telling lies, we should remind ourselves how important it is to look at what the Bible says. Then we can

ignore the thoughts Satan puts in our heads about
Heaven not being an awesome place to live.

So how can we know what Heaven is like if we've never seen it?

What's your favorite fantasy book? *The Hobbit? The
Lord of the Rings? A Wrinkle in Time?* What's your
favorite fantasy series? The Chronicles of Narnia?
The Pendragon series? In many fantasy books,
you can "see" the world described, because of the
author's vivid imagination. Yet places like Middle-
earth and Narnia don't really exist. (Don't you wish
they did?)

Heaven isn't a fantasy world based on someone's imagination. It's a real place created by God.
Yet many people believe it's impossible to know
anything about this place.

When I mentioned to a friend I was writing a book on Heaven, he told me, "God's Word
says that 'No eye has seen, no ear has heard, and
no mind has imagined what God has prepared
for those who love him.'" (He was quoting a
Bible verse, 1 Corinthians 2:9.)

"So what will you be talking about?" he asked.

"We can't really know what God has prepared for us in Heaven."

Maybe you've thought about the same thing. How *can* we know anything about Heaven—a place we can't see? It's this simple: God tells us about Heaven in the Bible. My friend stopped quoting too soon, because verse 10 of 1 Corinthians 2 says this about what we haven't seen or heard: "But it was to us that God revealed these things by his Spirit." So God has revealed unseen things to us in his Word, including things about Heaven.

God doesn't want us to shrug our shoulders as if there is no point in trying to learn about Heaven. Instead, he wants us to pay attention to what the Bible says about this amazing place so we'll look forward to what he has for us.

Of course, there are many things about Heaven we won't know until we get there. That's cool, don't you think? On Earth there are good surprises and bad surprises, but in Heaven God will give us only good surprises. And he has a lot of them waiting for us. I'm looking forward to them. How about you?

If we're good, does that mean we'll go to Heaven someday?

Many people believe that everyone who is good will wind up in Heaven. But the Bible says no one can be good enough to get there. We've all messed up (this is called *sin*). Like Edmund, who is addicted to the Witch's Turkish Delight in *The Lion, the Witch and the Wardrobe*, we get addicted to sin. It becomes a habit for us to do wrong things to get what we want, even though these things don't satisfy us. (Just like the Turkish Delight doesn't satisfy Edmund, but he keeps wanting it anyway.)

Because God is so good and does only what's right, he cannot stand sin. The Bible says that "the wages of sin is death" (Romans 6:23). Based on that verse, here's how the Narnia book puts it when Edmund sins:

> "You have a traitor there, Aslan," said the Witch. Of course everyone present knew that she meant Edmund. . . . "Have you forgotten the Deep Magic?" asked the Witch.

> "Let us say I have forgotten it," answered Aslan gravely. "Tell us of this Deep Magic."

"Tell you?" said the Witch, her voice growing
suddenly shriller. "Tell you what is written on
that very Table of Stone which stands beside
us? . . . You at least know the Magic which the
Emperor put into Narnia at the very beginning. You know that every traitor belongs to
me as my lawful prey and that for every treachery I have a right to a kill."

Every sinner deserves to die, and we are all sinners.
When you read about Edmund or watch the movie,
remind yourself that he isn't the only one who
deserves to die for his sins. We all do.

One of the good creatures of Narnia challenges
the Witch and her followers to a fight, to keep them
from killing Edmund for his sin. Here is the Witch's
response, followed by Aslan's:

"Fool," said the Witch with a savage smile that
was almost a snarl, "do you really think your
master can rob me of my rights by mere force?
He knows the Deep Magic better than that.
He knows that unless I have blood as the Law
says, all Narnia will be overturned and perish
in fire and water."

"It is very true," said Aslan, "I do not deny it."

The Bible tells us something very much like this in Hebrews 9:22: "According to the law of Moses . . . without the shedding of blood, there is no forgiveness."

The magic written on the Stone Table is the same as the law of God written on the stone tablets given to Moses. Unless someone who is pure and righteous sheds blood, no forgiveness for sins may be granted and no one may go to Heaven. This is not the devil's idea, just as it is not the White Witch's. It is God's holy character that requires it.

After hearing that Edmund has to die for his sins, his sister Lucy asks Aslan, "Can anything be done to save Edmund?"

Aslan's response is powerful: "All shall be done. . . . But it may be harder than you think." Then Aslan becomes very sad. Why? He knows the terrible suffering and death that await him. It is the only way to save Edmund.

Jesus experienced this very thing in the garden of Gethsemane. He told his disciples, "My soul is crushed with grief to the point of death. Stay here and keep watch with me" (Matthew 26:38).

Those serving the White Witch roll Aslan over on his back and tie his paws together, cheering as though they're being brave. Lewis adds, "Had the Lion chosen, one of those paws could have been the death of them all." Jesus said when he was arrested that he could have called on God, his Father in Heaven, to send over 72,000 angels for his protection (Matthew 26:53).

If you had the power to do that, wouldn't you have called on those angels in a heartbeat? I would have. But Jesus didn't. That's how much he loves us—because, remember, he went to the cross to save us.

Aslan makes no noise, just as Jesus didn't (Matthew 26:63). Even though Aslan's enemies tighten the cords so they cut into his flesh, he doesn't fight them.

The soldiers who held Jesus mocked him and hit him (Luke 22:63). In the same way, the Witch orders that Aslan, their rightful king, be shaved. They cut off his beautiful mane, then mock him, saying, "How many mice have you caught today, Cat?"

Aslan is willing to give his life for Edmund in the story. Jesus went to the cross to die for us, not just in a story, but in actual history. And he loves each of us enough that he would have died for us even if you or I were the only one who needed him.

Do you feel like thanking him for loving you that much? Go ahead. You can do it right now. . . .

Fortunately, the story didn't end with Christ's death. He came back to life in his same body. (This is what is called the "Resurrection.") His resurrection is very important to our Christian faith. And it's the key that unlocks our understanding of Heaven and what it will be like.

Will we have real bodies in Heaven?

To understand what the Heaven we'll live in is like, it's necessary to understand what *we* will be like.

Fish don't live on land; they live in water. People don't live in doghouses or in gerbil cages. Your bedroom wasn't made for an elephant to sleep in—especially not on the top bunk.

Since Christ promised he is preparing a

place *for us*, we should expect Heaven to be
perfectly suited to the kind of people we'll be.

Good news. The Bible tells us what we will
be like when we live in Heaven forever. After
Jesus returns, God will put back together the
bodies of his people who died, even thousands
of years earlier, and make them into strong and
healthy bodies. Our bodies will be like Christ's
body after he rose from the dead. The Bible says
Jesus will change our bodies "into glorious bodies
like his own" (Philippians 3:21).

So by knowing what *Christ's* resurrection body
was like, we know what *ours* will be like. The risen
Christ said to his followers, "Look at my hands.
Look at my feet. You can see that it's really me.
Touch me and make sure that I am not a ghost,
because ghosts don't have bodies, as you see that I
do" (Luke 24:39). Jesus had a physical body people
could touch and see. He ate with his disciples and
walked on Earth. We'll do those things on the New
Earth.

In *The Lion, the Witch and the Wardrobe*, after
Aslan is killed, he comes back to life and tells the
children just what the risen Jesus told his disciples.

"Aren't you dead then, dear Aslan?" said Lucy.

"Not now," said Aslan.

"You're not—not a—?" asked Susan in a shaky voice. She couldn't bring herself to say the word *ghost*. Aslan stooped his golden head and licked her forehead. The warmth of his breath and a rich sort of smell that seemed to hang about his hair came all over her.

"Do I look it?" he said.

"Oh, you're real, you're real! Oh, Aslan!" cried Lucy, and both girls flung themselves upon him and covered him with kisses.

You can imagine how glad the children are that Aslan has come back to life. That should help you envision how glad the disciples were when Jesus came back to life! They could hardly believe it.

Aslan is a picture of Jesus, the true Son of the Great Emperor, God the Father. And Aslan dying for Edmund's sins is a picture of Jesus dying for all our sins. Aslan coming back to life is a picture of Jesus' resurrection.

Remember, the Bible says that Jesus came back to life after he died. And in the day of resurrection, we will come back to life after we've died. Just like Jesus had a real body his followers could touch, we will have real bodies.

Will we have a good time in our resurrected bodies? Of course! After he came back to life, Jesus ate and drank with his disciples. In the book *The Lion, the Witch and the Wardrobe*, Aslan leaps over the children's heads after his resurrection, then dives between them, then picks them up and tosses them in the air with his huge "velveted paws" and catches them. They roll and laugh.

Lewis writes:

> It was such a romp as no one has ever had except in Narnia; and whether it was more like playing with a thunderstorm or playing with a kitten Lucy could never make up her mind.

Then Aslan warns the girls to put their fingers in their ears, and he roars ferociously, and all the trees bend before the blast.

That is a great picture of the power of Christ's resurrection—and of how real and powerful Christ's resurrection body is. Our resurrection bodies will be every bit as real!

After rejoicing at Aslan's resurrection, the children are still trying to figure out what it all means.

"It means," said Aslan, "that though the Witch knew the Deep Magic, there is a magic deeper still which she did not know. Her knowledge goes back only to the dawn of Time. But if she could have looked a little further back, into the stillness and the darkness before Time dawned, she would have read there a different incantation. She would have known that when a willing victim who had committed no treachery was killed in a traitor's stead, the Table would crack and Death itself would start working backwards."

The words *magic* and *incantation* refer to God's ancient laws. Christ not only died for our sins but conquered death for us by defeating it in his resurrection. So even when we die, death will not keep us from living forever with new, strong and healthy bodies!

Can we be sure we'll go to Heaven instead of Hell?

Think of Edmund in Narnia. He truly deserves to die. There is nothing Edmund can do to save his life. It is a gift from Aslan. No one goes to Heaven based on his or her good deeds. We get there only as a gift from Jesus.

In the Narnia story, do you see why Aslan's death on the Stone Table is necessary to save Edmund? In the real world, do you see why Christ's death on the cross was necessary to save *you*?

God gives us the opportunity to tell him, "I'm sorry for my sins." He allows us to choose whether or not to trust in Jesus. Repenting of our sins and trusting in Jesus and what he did for us is the only way to make Heaven our future home. Aslan's sacrifice for Edmund in *The Lion, the Witch and the Wardrobe* helps us understand what the Bible says in Romans about us deserving to die for our sins and Christ dying in our place:

> God has shown us a way to be made right with him . . . as was promised in the writings of Moses and the prophets long ago. We are made right with God by placing our faith in

Jesus Christ. And this is true for everyone who
believes, no matter who we are. For everyone
has sinned; we all fall short of God's glorious
standard. Yet God, with undeserved kindness,
declares that we are righteous. He did this
through Christ Jesus when he freed us from
the penalty for our sins. For God presented
Jesus as the sacrifice for sin. People are made
right with God when they believe that Jesus
sacrificed his life, shedding his blood. (Romans
3:21-25)

Christ offers everyone the gift of forgiveness, salvation, and eternal life. "Whoever is thirsty, let him
come; and whoever wishes, let him take the free
gift of the water of life" (Revelation 22:17, niv).

Eternal life is living joyfully with God forever.

Do you know what *salvation* means? It's
being rescued from eternal punishment for our
sins. Because Jesus paid the price for our sins on
the cross, we can be saved from Hell, and God
can take us to Heaven.

Notice Jesus calls it a "free gift." That means
we can't earn it: "God saved you by his grace when
you believed. And you can't take credit for this; it

is a gift from God. Salvation is not a reward for
the good things we have done, so none of us can
boast about it" (Ephesians 2:8-9).

Jesus came "so that by his death he might
destroy him who holds the power of death—
that is, the devil—and free those who all their
lives were held in slavery by their fear of death"
(Hebrews 2:14-15, NIV).

What delivers us from the fear of death? Only
a relationship with Jesus, who died in our place and
has gone to prepare a place for us in Heaven.

Heaven is a very special place for people to
go when they die. That is not true of the place
called Hell. It's a terrible place, and Jesus, more
than anyone else in the Bible, warned about it.
God doesn't live in Hell and never will. Since
God is the giver of all that's good, nothing good
will ever be there. No God, no good. It's that
simple.

People go to Hell because of their sins. The
bad news is, because everyone is a sinner, Hell is
the place where people automatically go when
they die if they've never asked Jesus to forgive
their sins.

The good news is that no one *has* to go to

Hell. Do you know what the *default setting* is in a computer program? It's what the computer will do unless something's done to change it. God loved us enough to make it possible to override the default setting of sin that would send us to Hell. Jesus died for us, taking the blame for our sins. He allowed himself to be given the death sentence on the cross so that we don't have to go to Hell. Instead, we can be with him in Heaven. That's how much he loves us!

But it's not enough to know these facts. We need to be sure we take God up on his offer of forgiveness. We need to accept—with thanks—his free gift of eternal life, so we can live forever with Jesus. Then we can know for sure that when we die, we will go to Heaven. (For more on this, look at chapter ten.)

What does it mean to store up treasure in Heaven?

Got a savings account, or maybe a bank in your room? You deposit money because you want to save for something important that you want to buy in the future. When you have a goal—something you'd like to do that's really important to you—your life is affected by it. If you're saving for a bike or a digital camera, you probably won't spend money on other things until you accomplish your goal. You'll deposit your money in your bank or your savings account.

Did you know that you can make deposits in Heaven? Jesus said, "Don't store up treasures here on earth, where moths eat them and rust destroys them, and where thieves break in and steal. Store your treasures in heaven, where moths and rust cannot destroy, and thieves do not break in and steal" (Matthew 6:19-20).

So, what's that all about? Well, many people work only to buy more and more things. But when we die, we won't be able to take any of our things with us to Heaven. Now, having possessions isn't *wrong*. But God wants people to be even more interested in the things that will last beyond this life.

What *will* last beyond this life? Our relationships with Jesus and other people who love him will be treasures that last forever. We also store up treasure in Heaven when we contribute to God's work on Earth.

God likes it when we do things for others, instead of spending all of our time and money on

ourselves. We can help older people, give money
to assist the poor, buy Bibles for people in China,
or give Christmas presents to children of prisoners.
We can give money so missionaries are able to fly
to different places and tell others about Jesus. We
can also use our talents to share God's love with
other people (like putting on a play to tell Jesus'
story to our neighbors, our families, or a group
of younger kids). If we do these things because
we love Jesus, a treasure will be waiting for us in
Heaven.

Remember how Jesus said that what we store
up on Earth will be moth eaten and rusty, but what
we store up in Heaven will be safe in God's hands?
By giving and sharing and doing things for Jesus
now, we can store up lasting treasures that will be
waiting for us when we get to Heaven.

Since the things we spend money on here
won't last, it's silly just to buy tons of things like
computers and stereos and toys that we end up setting aside anyway. (They don't make us happy, and
they just wind up getting sold in garage sales or on
eBay.) It's not only right but it's smart to share and
give money and food and other things to people
who really need them.

In addition to giving money to our church and to missionaries, we can give to Christian groups that help feed people who are hungry or have gone through disasters like floods, hurricanes, and earthquakes. Jesus wants us to do these things, and he will reward us for all we do.

I have a suggestion for a family field trip that you can discuss with your parents if you think it's a good idea: Visit a junkyard or a dump. The lines are shorter than in amusement parks, and admission is usually free! What's helpful is that you get to look at all the piles of "treasures" that were formerly Christmas and birthday presents. You will see stuff that people paid hundreds of dollars for, that children quarreled about, and that families went broke over. You might see arms and legs from battered dolls, rusted robots, and electronic gadgets lying useless and forgotten. You can be sure that much of the stuff you own will end up in a dump just like this.

Think ahead to a time when all that you ever owned will be in a junk heap. What will you have done that will last for eternity?

If you've learned to obey Jesus and store up your treasures in Heaven, the answer is exciting. Because if your treasures are in Heaven, then instead of spending your life headed *away* from your treasures, you'll be spending your life headed *toward* your treasures.

The more treasures you have in Heaven, the more you'll look forward to going there!

Chapter 2

AFTER WE DIE,
THEN WHAT?

Jesus replied, "I assure you, today you will be with me in paradise."

LUKE 23:43

The sweet air grew suddenly sweeter. A brightness flashed behind them. All turned. Tirian turned last because he was afraid. There stood his heart's desire, huge and real, the golden Lion, Aslan himself, and already the others were kneeling in a circle round his forepaws and burying their hands and faces in his mane as he stooped his great head to touch them with his tongue. Then he fixed his eyes upon Tirian, and Tirian came near, trembling, and flung himself at the Lion's feet, and the Lion kissed him and said, "Well done."

C. S. LEWIS, *The Last Battle*

What happens to us the second after we die?

In the movie *The Lord of the Rings: The Fellowship of the Ring*, there is a scene toward the end where Samwise Gamgee is drowning. He sees a bright light—usually a sign in movies and books that someone is dying. Why the light? Some people who claim to have had a near-death experience say they saw a bright light.

Death is a mystery because dead people don't usually come back and talk about life on the other side. (Well, there was Lazarus, the guy Jesus brought back to life in John 11. But the Bible never mentions what he had to say about death.)

There are some things we *can* know, based on what the Bible says. After we die, we don't cease to exist. *We live on, but in another location.* Followers of Jesus go to live with him in Heaven. While dying on the cross, Jesus told the thief crucified next to him, "Today you will be with me in paradise" (Luke 23:43). Obviously, Jesus knew that life after death was a reality.

Most of this book is about the future Heaven, where we will live forever with God and all those who know God. That's the place where we will live after our resurrection and after the end of this present Earth. What do I mean by *our resurrection*? When Jesus returns to Earth—and he promises he will someday—everyone who knows God and has died throughout the centuries will be given a new body. (More on that in chapter six.)

Usually when we refer to "Heaven," we're not thinking about that future Heaven where we'll live with Jesus on the New Earth. Most often we mean the *present* Heaven, the place where Christians go as soon as they die. When your parents tell you, "Your great-grandma's now in Heaven," they mean the present Heaven, as it is now.

The present Heaven, however, is *not* our final destination. Though it's a wonderful place, it's not the place we are made for—the place where God promises we can live forever. The future Heaven that will last forever is actually called something you might not expect. Have you noticed the phrase I've already used several times? It's called *the New Earth*. (More on that in chapter four.)

What's the difference between the present Heaven and the future Heaven?

Good question. The present Heaven is where angels live and where people go as soon as they die. Remember, it's a great place. The Bible says that to die and be with Christ "is even better" (Philippians 1:21) than being here now, even if we have a life that we really like.

The future Heaven will eventually be the home of God's people who are now living either on Earth or in the present Heaven. The coolest thing about this is that *God* will live with us there too!

John, one of Jesus' twelve chosen followers, saw a vision of the future Heaven. He said, "I saw a new heaven and a new earth, for the old heaven and the old earth had disappeared. . . . I heard a loud shout from the throne, saying, 'Look, God's home is now among his people! He will live with them, and they will be his people'" (Revelation 21:1, 3).

Some might think that the New Earth shouldn't be called Heaven. But "Heaven" is whatever special place God decides to make his home. So if God chooses the New Earth as his dwelling place, that means the New Earth will be Heaven.

God tells us that his perfect plan is to "bring everything together under the authority of Christ—everything in heaven and on earth" (Ephesians 1:10). Whenever we pray, "Your kingdom come, your will be done on earth as it is in heaven," we are looking forward to the day when Heaven and Earth will be together, no longer separate from each other.

Jesus says about all people who want to be his followers, "My Father will love them, and we will come and make our home with each of them" (John 14:23). So, we can look forward to living with God on the New Earth. And that New Earth won't seem strange to us. It will be our home. It will be all the good things that we love about this earth except w-a-a-a-y better. After all, God made people to live on the earth. And the New Earth will be very much like this one, except without the bad things.

Is Heaven "up"? Where exactly *is* it?

When you think about God, do you imagine him living somewhere in the sky? Many people do. After all, when Jesus went to Heaven after his resurrection, he rose into the sky and then disappeared. Talk about an amazing sight!

The present Heaven is normally invisible to those living on Earth. However, unlike an imaginary friend a little kid might have, it's real—we just can't see it.

Sometimes humans are allowed glimpses of Heaven. After Jesus' resurrection, a man named Stephen became his follower and was stoned to death because of his faith in Jesus. When this happened, he saw Heaven: "Look, I see the heavens opened and the Son of Man standing in the place of honor at God's right hand!" (Acts 7:56). He didn't dream this. He actually *saw* it.

We don't know exactly where Heaven is. It may be part of our own universe, or it may be in a different one—the Bible doesn't tell us. (Another of God's excellent surprises!) If you've read or watched science fiction, you may know about "parallel universes." While those places don't necessarily exist, Heaven is real. It may be a universe next door that's normally hidden but sometimes opened. Wherever Heaven is, we know that Jesus is there, along with those who know Jesus and have already died. Someday, if we

love Jesus, we'll be there too. If he returns to this
world before we die, we'll meet him in the air.

If we die before Jesus comes back, will we have bodies in the present Heaven?

You may have read books or seen TV shows or
movies where people become ghosts after they die.
In Charles Dickens's *A Christmas Carol*, Ebenezer
Scrooge sees the ghost of his dead partner, Jacob
Marley, plus three other ghosts—the Ghosts of
Christmas Past, Present, and Yet To Come. What
a terrible night that was!

Some people believe that Heaven is a place
full of ghostly figures floating around. But that's
not what the Bible teaches.

The truth is, humans are not meant to be ghosts
or spirits without bodies. When God created the first
human—Adam—he gave him a body. When God
breathed into Adam and gave him life, he was giving
him a spirit. We cannot be fully human without both
a spirit *and* a body.

So it's possible that God may give us some
temporary physical form while we wait for the final
resurrection. That's when all people who have died

will come back to life. At that point, everyone will be given a new body—one that will last forever. (Can't imagine that? Don't worry. God can. And he's the one in charge—aren't you glad?)

Remember, even after Jesus' resurrection, he had a body on Earth.

Jesus told a story in Luke 16:19-31 about two men who died: the rich man and Lazarus. Jesus spoke of the rich man's thirst, his tongue, and Lazarus's finger. He talked about them as if they had physical forms. However, these forms were *not* their resurrection bodies.

There's no such thing as a one-at-a-time resurrection when each person dies. So even if we have temporary physical forms in the present Heaven, which is possible but not certain, that is no substitute for the coming resurrection. When Jesus returns to Earth, his people will be restored to the same bodies they had, which will then be strong and healthy and will never die again.

Do people in Heaven remember life on Earth?

What are the easiest times to remember? Happy times? Scary times? There are some memories you

probably want to hold on to and others you want
to forget—like my memory of my first day of high
school, when I tripped and fell on my face, right in
front of three girls who laughed at me.

The Bible shows us that in Heaven we'll
remember our lives on Earth. Revelation 6 mentions martyrs (people who were killed because
of their faith in Jesus). They clearly remembered
events from their lives on Earth, including their
suffering and deaths. If they remembered those
times, surely they had other memories as well.
In fact, we'll all likely remember much more in
Heaven than we do on Earth. Maybe we'll even
see how God and his angels helped us when we
didn't realize it.

In Heaven, those who went through hard
times on Earth will be comforted. If there were no
memory of bad things, we wouldn't need comfort-
ing, would we?

Speaking of remembering, every reward in
Heaven will serve as a reminder of our service for
God here. Jesus told a story about three servants
who were given money to invest for their master.
(That story is in Matthew 25:14-30.) When the
master returned, he rewarded two servants for the

way they invested his money. Just like that master,
Jesus notices the way we invest our time and talents,
and someday he will reward us. Our faithful acts of
love and kindness and service for Christ will never
be forgotten.

Someday we'll remember and have to explain
why we did everything we did. This is called the
Judgment—the time when all of us have to stand
before God and give a reason for our choices.

Those who know Jesus don't have to worry
about being sent to Hell on Judgment Day. Jesus
paid our way to Heaven when he died on the cross
and came back to life. And until he returns, he will
help us live for God if we ask him to. God forgives
our sins whenever we confess them (1 John 1:9).
But, in light of the Judgment Day, it's clear that the
choices we make now are very important. On that
special day, we want to have good memories of the
life we lived on Earth.

Can people in Heaven see what's happening on Earth?

Yes, people in Heaven have some idea of what's
going on here. They may not know or pay attention to *everything* that's happening (like the time

you slipped ice into your brother's pillowcase). But
the martyrs in Revelation 6 knew that God hadn't
yet brought judgment on those who killed them, so
it's likely that they knew many other things about
what's happening on Earth.

At the very least, if they aren't *seeing* events,
people in Heaven are *told* about events on Earth.
For example, there's the time when Babylon (a
name that represents an evil world power) is
brought down. An angel points to Earth and says,
"Rejoice over her, O heaven! Rejoice, saints and
apostles and prophets! God has judged her for the
way she treated you" (Revelation 18:20, niv).

When Moses and Elijah appeared on the
mountain with Jesus, they spoke "about his exodus
from this world, which was about to be fulfilled in
Jerusalem" (Luke 9:31). They seemed to know what
was up with Jesus: how he'd have to die soon. (And
surely they returned to Heaven remembering what
they'd discussed with Jesus on Earth.)

Hebrews 12:1 tells us we are surrounded by
a "huge crowd of witnesses," the believers who've
died and are now with Jesus in Heaven. They seem
to be cheering us on from Heaven.

Jesus, who is in Heaven, definitely knows

what's up, especially with his people. (See chapters 2 and 3 of Revelation.) Isn't it great to discover Jesus knows everything, sees everything, is in control, and is never taken by surprise? For one thing, it means that he'll never find out something about us a million years from now and say, "If I'd known you did that, I'd never have let you into Heaven!" Jesus has seen us at our worst and still loves us. And in Heaven he'll see to it that we'll always be at our best—and that's how we'll always want to be.

Are people in Heaven praying for people on Earth?

The answer is possibly yes—at least sometimes.

Jesus, who is both God and man, is in Heaven praying for people on Earth (Romans 8:34). So there's at least *one* human being who has died and gone to Heaven and is now praying for those on Earth. But it appears he may not be the only one praying. The martyrs, who died for their faith, are in Heaven praying for God's justice on the earth (Revelation 6:9-10). These prayers will affect

Christians who are mistreated because of their faith in Jesus. (Many are in prison around the world.)

The Bible doesn't specifically say whether the rest of the people in Heaven are praying about what's happening on Earth. But since prayer is simply talking to God, this suggests that we'll pray more in Heaven than we do now—not less.

HOW WILL WE RELATE
TO GOD IN HEAVEN?

*I know that my Redeemer lives, and that in the end he will
stand upon the earth. And after my skin has been destroyed, yet
in my flesh I will see God; I myself will see him with my
own eyes.*

Job 19:25-27, NIV

*As for Aslan himself, the Beavers and the children didn't know
what to do or say when they saw him. . . . For when they tried
to look at Aslan's face they just caught a glimpse of the golden
mane and the great, royal, solemn, overwhelming eyes; and
then they found they couldn't look at him and went all
trembly.* (Chapter 12)

*And so the girls did what they would never have dared to do without
his permission, but what they had longed to do ever since they first
saw him—buried their cold hands in the beautiful sea of fur and
stroked it and, so doing, walked with him.* (Chapter 14)

C. S. Lewis, *The Lion, the Witch and the Wardrobe*

Will we actually see God?

Think about the person you would most want to
spend time with. Who would that person be? Your
favorite singer, author, or athlete? Your best friend
who moved away? A family member who's already
died?

Many Christians would say they'd want to
spend time with Jesus. They'd want to see the
Savior who created them, died for them, and
made their life in Heaven possible—the one
who loves them more than anyone else.

During his Sermon on the Mount, Jesus said,
"God blesses those whose hearts are pure, for they

will see God" (Matthew 5:8). So that means yes,
we'll see God. But Jesus also said, "God is Spirit"
(John 4:24). By this he meant that God the Father
doesn't have a body. But Jesus, God's Son, does.
And because Jesus is God himself, to see Jesus will
be to see God.

Isaiah, an Old Testament prophet, had a vision
of God. "He was sitting on a lofty throne, and the
train of his robe filled the Temple" (Isaiah 6:1).
Isaiah knew that the great and awesome God was
seated on a throne. He didn't have to be told, "Hey,
that's God."

Seeing God made Isaiah afraid—just like Peter,
Susan, Lucy, and Mr. and Mrs. Beaver "went all
trembly" when they saw Aslan.

We can't blame Isaiah for his fear, any more
than the children in Narnia, because people usually don't see God. Even the sight of an angel will
terrify people. (See Daniel 10:7-10.) Perhaps Isaiah
thought of God's words to Moses, "You may not
look directly at my face, for no one may see me and
live" (Exodus 33:20). But God allowed Isaiah to see
him. In Heaven, we also will be allowed to see God
(Revelation 22:3-4).

The more time we spend with God, the better

we'll know him. He's by far the most fascinating
person in the universe. (After all, he's the one that
made all the interesting people we've ever known or
read about.) Think of the questions we'll be able to
ask God. Are you getting your list ready? I sure am!

When you get to know Jesus better, he'll be
at the very top of your list of people you'd want to
spend your day with. Sports and movie celebrities
might be fun to meet, but they would get boring
pretty soon. Jesus will never bore us. And the great
thing is, you don't have to wait to be with him. You
can spend time with him right now. You do this by
reading his Word (the Bible), praying to him, and
thanking him for being with you all day long.

What does *eternal life* mean?

There are some events in life that seem to go on
forever: the half hour before the end of school each
day (especially the last day of school), or the speech
you have to make in front of the whole class, or the
family dinner that takes so long for everyone to finish when you're waiting to eat dessert. And there
are some unbelievable moments—when you finally
learn to snowboard or win the game for your team

or get a hug from someone you love—that you wish *would* last forever. While none of these events actually lasts forever, eternal life does. It wouldn't be called *eternal* if it didn't.

Jesus said, "For God loved the world so much that he gave his one and only Son, so that everyone who believes in him will not perish but have eternal life" (John 3:16). This never-ending life is promised to those who believe in Jesus. "But how can this be?" you might ask. "After all, everyone will die at some point." True. But death isn't the end of the story. Jesus promised that someday we'll live forever with him. That means we'll live again after we die.

As a promise that this will happen, we have the Holy Spirit. Jesus told his followers that the Holy Spirit would come and make his home within every person who believes in Jesus. (Don't just take my word for it. Read John 14:15-17, 26.) We're told about God's guarantee in Ephesians 1:14: "The Spirit is God's guarantee that he will give us the inheritance he promised." That inheritance, which we will receive as God's children, is eternal life.

Eternal life is more than an existence that never ends. It's a quality life that's filled with joy.

In the Star Trek movie *Generations*, Guinan

tells Captain Picard about a place called the Nexus. She describes it this way: "It was like being inside joy, as if joy was something tangible and you could wrap yourself up in it like a blanket."

I don't believe in the Nexus. But I *do* believe in the new heavens and the New Earth. What will it be like there? Like "being inside joy, as if joy were something tangible and you could wrap yourself up in it like a blanket."

How will we worship God?

What do you think *worship* means? Singing to God? Going to church? Some people have an idea that worshipping God is boring, something you *have* to do. They forget, or really aren't sure, how awesome God is. They think of Heaven as a long church service. Ever think that way?

You'd probably wait all day to see your favorite celebrity if you knew that he or she was soon to appear at your local mall or bookstore. No one would have to drag you there. You'd *want* to see that person! And when you saw that person, what would you say? Probably something like, "Wow, I'm so-o-o glad to meet you!" You'd probably name something you appreciate about the person—his book; her tennis serve; the cool way he played the invading alien general in his last movie.

Even if you are nervous, no one has to tell you to say something nice to a celebrity you've met. In the same way, no one will have to tell you in Heaven, "Say something nice to God." You'll just naturally do it and want to do it and *enjoy* doing it. Worship simply means expressing your appreciation for God.

Some might wonder if all we'll do in Heaven is worship God. Well, yes and no. *No*, because the Bible says we'll be doing many other things—eating, working, relaxing, learning, etc. And *yes,* because all that we do will show our appreciation for God in acts of worship that will never end.

Worship involves more than singing and prayer. We're commanded, "Always be joyful. Never stop praying. Be thankful in all circumstances" (1 Thessalonians 5:16-18). We know that God expects us to do many different things on Earth, such as work, rest, and spend time with our families. So if we are to be joyful, pray, and give thanks all the time, we must worship God *even while doing other things.* Same deal in Heaven.

Why would God want to serve us in Heaven?

Have you read how Jesus washed the feet of his followers (John 13)? They were amazed that a leader and teacher they respected so much would do the work of a servant. Peter especially couldn't bear the thought of Jesus doing that. But Jesus insisted on washing his friends' feet.

Jesus also said, "The servants who are ready and waiting for his return will be rewarded. I tell you the truth, he himself will seat them, put on an apron, and serve them as they sit and eat!" (Luke 12:37).

Imagine being served by Jesus. Whoa! That's even greater than the president coming to your house and making a meal for you! If we came up with this idea ourselves, we'd be crazy! The Creator serving *us*? *Yeah, r-i-i-i-g-h-t.* But we didn't come up with the idea—God did!

We owe him everything. He owes us nothing. But that doesn't keep God from choosing to serve us, his servants. Jesus served us when he died for us. He said about himself, "For even the Son of Man came not to be served but to serve others and to give his life as a ransom for many" (Matthew 20:28).

As a father who loves his children goes out of his way to help them, God promises that he will always give of himself for us. Why? Because he loves us and wants to show forever his appreciation for our loyalty and service to him in this life. Does that mean we deserve God's grace? Of course not. By definition, God's grace is something we don't deserve. If we deserved it, it wouldn't be grace!

Somehow, in his great love for us, our King becomes a servant, making us (his servants) kings! Notice that he won't merely command his *other* servants to serve us. He will do it himself. That's why the grace we sing about in church is called "*Amazing* Grace." If you think about it, there's nothing more amazing than God's love for us.

Doesn't that make you want to love him more and more every day?

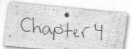

WHAT IS THE NEW EARTH? WHAT WILL IT BE LIKE?

Then I saw a new heaven and a new earth. . . . And I heard a loud voice from the throne saying, "Now the dwelling of God is with men, and he will live with them. They will be his people, and God himself will be with them and be their God. . . ." [Jesus] said, "I am making everything new!"

REVELATION 21:1, 3, 5, NIV

Wrong will be right, when Aslan comes in sight,
At the sound of his roar, sorrows will be no more,
When he bares his teeth, winter meets its death,
And when he shakes his mane, we shall have
spring again.

C. S. LEWIS, *The Lion, the Witch and the Wardrobe*

Is God going to destroy the earth and make a different one from scratch?

For some, the destruction of the earth is something that only happens in science fiction books and movies. But Peter, one of Jesus' twelve disciples, wrote about what will really happen someday: "The heavens will pass away with a terrible noise, and the very elements themselves will disappear in fire, and the earth and everything on it will be found to deserve judgment" (2 Peter 3:10). Sounds scary, huh? (But if you know Jesus, you can relax, because "the end" will be followed by a fantastic new beginning of an exciting life that will go on forever!)

Some Bible teachers think that the earth will be completely destroyed and a different Earth will be made from scratch. But the Bible teaches us that while the earth will be destroyed for a while, it will be restored. God will make the same old Earth into the New Earth, which will be better than it ever was!

Think about the Flood that happened during the time of Noah. Although the earth seemed to be destroyed, it really wasn't. It continued to exist.

We know the Bible says our bodies will die, but God will bring the same bodies back to life in a much better condition. In the same way, the earth will die, but God will bring it back in a much better condition. That will be the New Earth.

You could compare the earth's future changes to that of a caterpillar. As you know, major changes happen to a caterpillar after it goes into a chrysalis. It comes out a new creature—a butterfly. It hasn't stopped existing. It's the same, yet transformed. And it's a real, lasting transformation. Though Transformer action figures can be changed back and forth, the butterfly can't be changed back to a caterpillar (nor would it want to be). Likewise, the New Earth will never change back to the old Earth.

When God fashions this earth so that it's new again, we're going to live with him on it. Remember, Jesus was a carpenter. What do carpenters do? They *make* things, and they *fix* things that are broken. This earth is broken. It's far from perfect now because of sin. But Jesus is going to fix it, just like he's going to fix us. We will be the same people made new, and we will live on the same Earth made new.

Pretty exciting, don't you think?

Will the New Earth be like our Earth was in the beginning?

What's the most beautiful place you've ever seen or hope to see? What makes it beautiful to you? The Garden of Eden was probably the most beautiful place that ever existed. After all, the first people God created lived there in the days before pollution or earthquakes or wars or poverty or crime. We can only imagine what it was like.

Every beautiful place on Earth—the Grand Canyon, the Alps, the Amazon rain forests, the Serengeti Plain in Tanzania (where lions roam)— is just a small taste of what the New Earth will be like.

It's like when your mom or dad lets you have a tiny piece of turkey or dressing to sample just before the Thanksgiving meal. It's not enough to satisfy you, but it's good enough to help you think about how delicious the whole meal will be!

All our lives, even if we don't know it, we've been dreaming of the New Earth—the Heaven that will last forever. Whenever we see beauty in water, wind, flower, animal, man, woman, or child, we see just a sample of what Heaven will be like.

We should expect this New Earth to be like
the Garden of Eden, only better. That's exactly what
the Bible promises: "The LORD will comfort Israel
again. . . . Her desert will blossom like Eden, her
barren wilderness like the garden of the LORD. Joy
and gladness will be found there. Songs of thanksgiving will fill the air" (Isaiah 51:3).

Will places like the Grand Canyon actually be on the New Earth?

Ever see an old house, car, or painting fixed up to
look the way it used to be (before age and wear and
tear messed it up)? Houses and cars are restored
every day. Even paintings by famous artists from
centuries ago have been restored. Sometimes an artist or a team of artists cleans and (if necessary) uses
new paint to brighten the faded colors of an old
painting. Although the painting is still the same, it
looks once again like it was meant to look.

The New Earth will still be Earth just as we,
in our new bodies, will still be ourselves. So we
can expect New Earth's sky to be blue and its grass
green. Lake Louise (in Alberta, Canada) will likely
become New Lake Louise.

In *The Last Battle*, when the children enter Aslan's Country from Narnia, though they don't yet know it's Heaven, they see familiar sights not only from Narnia but from their earth as well. Suddenly Peter says, "It's England. And that's the house itself—Professor Kirke's old home in the country where all our adventures began!"

Edmund reminds him that the house had been destroyed. But then he's told, "So it was. . . . But you are now looking at the England within England, the real England just as this is the real Narnia. And in that inner England no good thing is destroyed."

Then Peter, Edmund, and Lucy gasp and shout and wave because across a valley they see their father and mother!

We will meet all kinds of new people and see all kinds of new places—but we will also see familiar people and familiar places, because we will be with resurrected people we love on the resurrected Earth we love.

Based on what the Bible says, I think we'll not only see things the way they are now, but we'll see things the way they were meant to be. On the New Earth, no good thing will be destroyed. Everything

we love about the old Earth will be ours on the
New Earth—either in the same form or another.
Once we understand this, we won't regret leaving
all the cool places we've seen or wish we'd seen.
Why? *Because we know we'll see many of them on the
New Earth—and they will be better than ever!*

What will the New Jerusalem be like?

What's the most beautiful city you've ever seen?
Some would say Victoria in British Columbia.
Others might name Savannah, Georgia, with its
many gardens, or San Francisco, California, for
the Golden Gate Bridge. Still others say London
or Shanghai or Paris or Florence. These cities are
pretty cool. (I happen to love Portland, Oregon,
where I was born, and close to where I still live.)

But the most beautiful city anyone will ever
see will be New Jerusalem. You might have seen
pictures of the old Jerusalem in Sunday school or
in a Bible with pictures. But on the New Earth,
New Jerusalem will be the capital city—the largest
city that has ever existed. It will be a huge garden city.

In the book of Revelation, John describes the

city: "The wall was made of jasper, and the city of
pure gold, as pure as glass. The foundations of the
city walls were decorated with every kind of precious stone" (Revelation 21:18-19, NIV). John also
writes that each gate was carved from a single, huge
pearl (verse 21). Can you imagine how magnifi-
cent that will be? There will be more wealth in this
immense city than has been gathered in all human
history. Everyone will be free to enjoy it, and no
one will ever fight over it or try to keep it from
others. We'll all be glad to share everything we
have and everything we find.

An angel tells John that the New Jerusalem
is 1,400 miles in length, width, and height (Revelation 21:15-16). A city this size in the middle
of the United States would stretch from Canada
to Mexico and from the Appalachian Mountains
to the California border! And it will be that high
too! Now that is really huge. We sure won't have
to worry about overcrowding!

It appears there will be many other cities on
New Earth, since Jesus said that in the Kingdom
some would rule over five cities and some over ten
(Luke 19:17, 19). But no city will be like this great
capital city—and there on Main Street, in the cen-

ter of the city, will be "the throne of God" and his
Son, Jesus, the King of kings (Revelation 22:1-2).

What is the River of Life?

Quick! Name a liquid you drink when you're
really, really thirsty. "Is this a trick question?" you
might wonder. No, there's no trick. The answer, of
course, is water. (In fact, every other drink you like
is mostly water anyway.) The New Jerusalem will
have plenty of water—and this water will flow from
the River of Life.

John describes it as "a river with the water of
life, clear as crystal, flowing from the throne of God
and of the Lamb. It flowed down the center of the
main street" (Revelation 22:1-2). Why will water
be important in the New Jerusalem? Because the
city will be a center of human life, and water is an
important part of life.

Ghosts don't need water, but human bodies
do. We all know what it's like to be thirsty, but
the people who lived in Israel during Bible times
really knew the importance of water. After all,
they lived in a bone-dry climate.

A river is a good source for fresh water. Why?

Because it continually moves and changes. Think of the Mississippi or the Colorado River.

The River of Life may have numerous off-shoots flowing throughout the rest of the city. Can you picture people talking and laughing beside this river, sticking their hands and faces down into the water and drinking? Perhaps we'll travel in gondolas throughout the city like many people do in Venice, Italy!

What is the Tree of Life?

Think about your favorite kind of tree. Has there ever been a tree that made you go, "Whoa"? Some people react that way to tall redwoods, giant sequoias, or bristlecone pine trees, which live for thousands of years.

The Bible mentions two amazing trees. Remember the Tree of Life and the tree of the knowledge of good and evil mentioned in Genesis? (If not, look at the story in Genesis 2:9, 15-17.) The second tree—the tree of the knowledge of good and evil—had fruit God told Adam and Eve *not* to eat. But they ate it anyway.

The first tree—the Tree of Life—used to be in Eden, but now it's in Heaven (Revelation 2:7). One

day it will be moved to the New Earth. John saw in
a vision what this tree will be like in the future: "On
each side of the river grew a tree of life, bearing
twelve crops of fruit, with a fresh crop each month"
(Revelation 22:2).

After Adam and Eve sinned, God stopped
them from eating fruit from the Tree of Life
(Genesis 3:22-23). If they had eaten this fruit,
they would have lived forever. "What's wrong
with that?" you might wonder. Well, they would
have lived forever away from God—unable to
come near him because of their disobedience.

You see, God is so holy that he cannot allow
sin in his presence: "Your eyes are too pure to look
on evil; you cannot tolerate wrong" (Habakkuk 1:13,
NIV).

Disobedience often resulted in death in Old
Testament times. That's why the people of Israel
had to offer animal sacrifices. It was a picture of
the coming Messiah, Jesus, who would die for the
sins of all people. Jesus never disobeyed God, his
heavenly Father. So when he died on the cross, he
was the perfect sacrifice, ending the need for animal
sacrifices.

Let's get back to the Tree of Life. What's cool

about it is that eating the fruit from it—and somehow making use of its leaves—may be a way of giving us new energy every day, preventing sickness of any kind, and keeping us well forever. Its leaves will be used as medicine the way many plants are used today (like the aloe plant). Well, maybe not medicine as we think of it. After all, God promised that we won't feel pain or have illnesses on the New Earth. "He will wipe every tear from their eyes, and there will be no more death or sorrow or crying or pain" (Revelation 21:4).

What other cool features will the New Earth have?

If you get a new version of a computer game, you hope that the new version will have better features, don't you? You eagerly scan the package, hoping that you'll see phrases like *better graphics* or *a bigger adventure*.

It's only natural to wonder what new features "Earth version 2.0" will have, especially considering how the original Earth 1.0, once an amazingly good program, was infected with the Sin Virus on every level. The River of Life and the Tree of Life are just a couple of the fantastic things we'll see on New Earth. Because it will be a new version of this same Earth, we should expect some of the features we see now: forests, waterfalls, and rivers, for example.

In describing New Earth, John speaks of "a great, high mountain" (Revelation 21:10). Note that John calls it *a* mountain, not *the* mountain. We know that New Earth has at least one mountain. And since the New Earth is called "Earth," there's every reason to believe it will have hundreds or thousands of mountains, just like this earth, right? Just as our new bodies will be better than our current ones, the New Earth's natural wonders will be more spectacular than those we now see.

Will there be time on the New Earth?

Many people believe that there will be no such thing as time on New Earth. They point to this verse, written by Peter: "A day is like a thousand years to the Lord, and a thousand years is like a day" (2 Peter 3:8).

But notice it says "to the Lord." It doesn't say

"to human beings." Why? Because God has always existed (he is unlimited or infinite). But we had a beginning (we are limited or finite). He will always be the Creator, and we will always be creatures. God made us as physical and spiritual creatures to live in space and time.

Many people remember the phrase "time shall be no more" and think it's from the Bible. It's actually from an old hymn. That there is time in Heaven is made clear many places in the Bible:

- We're told "there was silence throughout heaven for about half an hour" (Revelation 8:1).

- Beings in Heaven relate to events as they happen on Earth, right down to rejoicing the moment a sinner on Earth repents (Luke 15:7).

- People in Heaven ask God "how long"; then they are told by God to "wait a little longer" (Revelation 6:10-11, NIV). These words refer to lengths of time.

- Those who live in Heaven sing (Revelation 5:9-13). Also, there are a number of references to musical instruments in Heaven. Meter, tempo, and rests are all essential components of music, and each is time related. Certain notes are held longer than others. Songs start and they finish. That means they take place in time. (Ask your piano teacher if music can exist without time.)

- The Tree of Life on New Earth will have "a fresh crop each month" (Revelation 22:2). A month is a measure of time.

When we have conversations in Heaven, they will have a beginning, a middle, and an end. All the words won't be spoken at once! (How weird would that be?) This means that we'll experience time in Heaven.

Some people get nervous or even scared about living forever. The idea of time going on and on bothers them. But that's because right now we are capable of getting tired and bored. So it naturally seems as if time that goes on forever would be boring. But the things that make us fearful of living forever will be completely gone. Once we're with the Lord, we'll be really excited to learn things *about* God and *from* God in a great new universe.

Time will always be our friend, never our enemy. We won't wish that time would slow down (like when we're having a great time laughing with family and friends at a pizza party) or speed up (like when we're waiting to ask Mom a question and she's on the phone). We won't be bored, and we won't have to stop doing what we love. Time in Heaven will always flow just right—it won't seem too long or too short!

WHO RULES?

The holy people of the Most High will be given the kingdom,
and they will rule forever and ever.

DANIEL 7:18

Down at Cair Paravel there are four thrones and it's a saying in
Narnia time out of mind that when two Sons of Adam and two
Daughters of Eve sit on those four thrones, then it will be the end
not only of the White Witch's reign but of her life.

C. S. LEWIS, *The Lion, the Witch and the Wardrobe*

Who will rule the New Earth?

Ever thought about running for president? Maybe
you thought you'd make a great president of your
class or even king or queen of your school. Whether
or not you're voted in, guess what—God has a leadership role in mind for you on the New Earth. He
might have you ruling a whole city someday.

Get this: Someday Jesus will be declared the
absolute ruler of the universe. He will turn over to
his Father the Kingdom he has won (1 Corinthians
15:28). Then God will give people the responsibil-
ity of ruling the New Earth (Revelation 22:5).

W-a-a-a-y back when God created the world,
he decided that humans should rule the earth: "God
blessed them and said, 'Be fruitful and multiply. Fill
the earth and govern it. Reign over the fish in the
sea, the birds in the sky, and all the animals that
scurry along the ground'" (Genesis 1:28).

Human kingdoms will begin and end until
Jesus sets up a kingdom that forever replaces them.

My wife, Nanci, and I were able to go to
London to attend the international premiere of *The
Lion, the Witch and the Wardrobe*. It was at the Royal
Albert Hall. Bright lights shone, artificial snow fell,
and television cameras were everywhere. People

crowded around to get autographs of the actors
and actresses. Afterward, we got to meet the director, the producer, and some of the cast. We leaned
against the lamppost from the movie, Nanci sat
on the White Witch's throne, and we ate Turkish
delight (but without the enchantment that would
have made us want more and more). It was a lot
of fun.

One unforgettable moment happened just
before the movie started. Charles, the Prince of
Wales, and his wife, Camilla, the Duchess of
Cornwall, walked into the Royal Box, just eighty
feet from us. Trumpet players announced their
entrance, and everyone stood and fixed their eyes
on them, to honor royalty.

The moment we sat down, the lights went out
and the movie started. The movie reminded me that
Jesus is the true King, an all-knowing monarch without faults, who is worthy of our complete adoration
and loyalty.

Though Aslan is the highest king in Narnia,
the "King of kings," he makes Peter, Edmund,
Susan, and Lucy kings and queens over his kingdom! Well, guess what? C. S. Lewis got that idea
right from the Bible. That's exactly what Jesus,

the King of kings, does: He appoints us as kings and queens to rule over his kingdom on the New Earth.

Jesus gives this promise in Matthew 25:34: "Come, you who are blessed by my Father, inherit the Kingdom prepared for you from the creation of the world." So, what is the inheritance you are to receive? Jesus says, "God blesses those who are humble, for they will inherit the whole earth" (Matthew 5:5). That means you're royalty—like the children in the Narnia stories. But have you read *The Silver Chair*? In that story a serpent, who's also a witch, puts Prince Rilian under her spell, so he forgets that he's really the prince of Narnia. In the same way, Satan doesn't want us to know who we are—the King's children, whom the King has appointed to rule his kingdom. (I'll say it again: *We're royalty!*)

How long will we rule?

How long will God's kingdom, which he will share with us, last on the New Earth? God gave the answer to the prophet Daniel in Daniel 7:18 as quoted at the beginning of this chapter: We "will rule forever and ever." We're not going to be royalty just a little while, but always.

The Narnia story says, "Once a king or queen in Narnia, always a king or queen." We also could say, "Once a king or queen on New Earth, always a king or queen."

Who will we rule?

We will rule, or lead, people like us. And angels, too. "Don't you realize that someday we believers will judge [rule over] . . . angels?" (1 Corinthians 6:2-3).

We will also rule animals, just like God told Adam and Eve to do in Genesis 1–2.

And who will rule over us? Other people. In any government, one person is in charge of numerous people. Those people are both over and under other people.

Here on the old Earth, where sin is still a problem, we may get angry with a brother or sister who tells us what to do. But someone leading us in Heaven won't bother us a bit. There will be no pride, envy, boasting, or any wrong attitudes.

All of us can serve God in some way. Maybe you help out with the younger kids at your church.

Or maybe you do kind deeds without having to be asked, such as cleaning up someone else's mess. Those who serve God now will be able to serve him on New Earth. The Bible says the humble servant will be put in charge of much, while the one who bosses everyone else around will have power taken away. Someone who tries to make others think he or she is important will be humbled. Someone who is humble and doesn't act important will be treated as if he or she *is* important (Luke 14:11).

On this earth, we sometimes think serving others is a chore. (C'mon. Admit it. Everyone thinks that way sometimes.) But on the New Earth, it won't be. And even now, we can honor Jesus and enjoy serving other people. How? By putting Jesus first, others second, and ourselves third: "Be humble, thinking of others as better than yourselves" (Philippians 2:3). This doesn't come naturally. But we can ask Jesus to help us do it! (Why not ask him right now?)

Will God create new worlds?

First, a history lesson. (This won't take long.) Know anything about Alexander the Great? He's an actual person who lived from 356–323 BC. At an early age he decided to take over the known world and managed to conquer the Persian Empire. He was cruel, deadly, and thorough. But even a conqueror runs out of places to conquer, especially if he can't create new worlds to take over. In spite of that, he had this idea that he was . . . well . . . a god. (Sorry, Alex! The real God has always had that job and always will.) Alexander died when he was only thirty-three. So much for being a god.

Jesus also died at about thirty-three—but he rose from the dead, because he really *is* God! He came back to life, never to die again. Nobody else has ever done that.

God the Father had this to say about his Son, the Savior: "Of the increase of his government and peace there will be no end" (Isaiah 9:7, niv). This means there will be no limit to his kingdom. The fact that his government will continue to increase forever suggests that God, the Creator, might make new worlds to expand his kingdom.

God is the original artist, and artists love to create. God didn't create the world and then retire from his work. Jesus said, "My Father is always at his work to this very day, and I, too, am working"

(John 5:17, NIV). We can't even imagine what he has already been doing—much less what he will do in the ages to come.

As God creates new things, he will probably continue to put us in charge of his creation. We'll have stuff to do, places to go, and people to see. We'll do things that bring joy to us and pleasure to God, our Creator and Father.

Chapter 6

WHAT WILL OUR LIVES IN HEAVEN BE LIKE?

*You will show me the way of life, granting me the joy
of your presence and the pleasures of living
with you forever.*

Psalm 16:11

Everyone raised his hand to pick the fruit he best liked
the look of, and then everyone paused for a second. This fruit
was so beautiful that each felt, "It can't be meant for me . . .
surely we're not allowed to pluck it."
"It's all right," said Peter. ". . . I've a feeling we've got to
the country where everything is allowed."

C. S. Lewis, *The Last Battle*

Will we become angels in Heaven?

Many people think that Heaven is a city of angels.
They have heard that everyone who goes there
receives a harp and halo, then sits on a cloud.

Some people believe that we'll become angels
because they misunderstand something Jesus said:
"When the dead rise, they will neither marry nor
be given in marriage. In this respect they will be
like the angels in heaven" (Matthew 22:30). But
Jesus was just talking about the fact that angels
don't get married. He wasn't saying that people
become angels, or even that we'll be like angels
in any other way besides not marrying.

So what's the answer to the question, "Will
we become angels in Heaven?" The answer is no.
When you go to live in Heaven, you will still be a
human being. Both angels and humans are intel-

ligent, and both were created to serve God, which gives their lives meaning and joy. But still, people and angels are very different. God is creative and loves variety. (Look at colors, flowers, and animals.) He doesn't make all intelligent creatures alike. (Hey, he doesn't even make any two snowflakes or fingerprints alike!)

Angels are beings with their own identities— with histories and memories. They have names, like Michael and Gabriel. Under God's direction, they serve us on Earth. Michael, the archangel, serves under God; and the other angels, in different positions, serve under Michael. In Heaven, human beings will be in charge of angels (1 Corinthians 6:2-3). How cool will that be?

Will we have feelings and express them?

Do you think God ever laughs or cries? In the Bible, God is said to enjoy, love, laugh, take delight, and rejoice, as well as be angry, jealous, and sad. We know that after Jesus' friend Lazarus died, "Jesus wept" (John 11:35—the shortest verse in the Bible). God also tells us that when the disciples tried to send some children away from Jesus, "he was angry with his disciples" (Mark 10:14).

We were made in God's image, so we have feelings and express them just as God does. We should expect to do the same in Heaven.

On Earth our feelings sometimes cause us to do wrong things. That's why many people have a hard time with their feelings. For example, anger can lead to hurting other people, or feeling hurt by them. In Heaven we'll all be free to feel deeply and never have to be afraid that our feelings will lead to hurtful actions by us or by others. We'll all love each other and never hurt each other's feelings.

I can hardly wait for that.

Will we be allowed to have or do what we really, really want?

Have you ever wanted something and been told, "You can't have it because it's bad for you"? Maybe you *really* wanted to eat sixteen scoops of ice cream instead of dinner. Or maybe you wanted to play video games all afternoon instead of doing your homework.

We'll have many desires in Heaven, but everything we want will be good. Our desires will please God. All will be right with the world, nothing off-limits.

When your mom or dad or Uncle Zach prepares steaks or burgers on the barbecue grill, the chef wants the family to hear the meat sizzle and look forward to eating it. God created our desires and all the things we long to have. He loves it when our mouths water for what he's prepared for us. When we enjoy looking forward to the gifts God has promised us, we're enjoying him.

One of the best things about Heaven is that the bad desires we had to fight on Earth won't be around anymore. We'll enjoy food without eating too much or too little, we won't do anything to hurt ourselves, and we won't do anything to hurt anyone else.

On the New Earth after Jesus comes back (see chapter four), there will no longer be a difference between what we *should* do and what we *want* to do.

Will we have the same identities we have now?

Great news! You will be *you* in Heaven.

Think about it. The risen Jesus did not become someone else; he was the same Jesus he had been before his resurrection. He said to his disciples: "You can see that it's really me" (Luke 24:39). Jesus dealt with Thomas and Peter in very personal ways because he knew a lot about them. When Thomas saw Jesus a week after the Resurrection, he said, "My Lord and my God!" (John 20:28). He knew he was speaking to the same Jesus he'd followed before Jesus' death on the cross. When John was fishing with some of the other disciples, he saw Jesus on the seashore and said, "It's the Lord!" (John 21:7). He meant, "It's really him—the Jesus we have known."

Our own personalities and histories will continue on from the old Earth to the New Earth. So you'll still recognize friends and family. They will recognize you, too. Best of all, Jesus will know you . . . and you will know him!

This also means you'll still be male (if you're a male) or female (if you're a female). While some people say that in Heaven we will no longer be male and female, the Bible doesn't say that. After all, when people looked at Jesus in his resurrection body, they knew he was still a man, not a woman.

What will our new bodies be like?

Ever wish you could look like someone else? Maybe you would like to be as tall as your brother or to have the same hair color as a friend. Perhaps you'd like to be able to do some things that others can do. You might think you'd be really happy if you could just play soccer as well as one of the other kids at school.

After Jesus comes back to this earth, we'll have new bodies for the New Earth. And what's awesome is that these bodies will be better than anything we can imagine! For one thing, they will be free of the curse that came upon Earth because of the first sin in the Garden of Eden. "No longer will there be a curse upon anything" (Revelation 22:3).

The curse is what removed beauty from God's creation, or hid beauty from our sight. So without the curse, everything and everyone God has made will be beautiful. And we will never fail to see that beauty in them. There will be no diseases, no handicaps—not even any skin problems.

Our bodies will all look good without the fake sort of beauty that is often found in movies and advertisements. After all, in some countries being thin is seen as unhealthy while a heavier build is a sign of strength and good health. But in Heaven no one will think of himself, herself, or anyone else as ugly or weird. (Imagine how cool *that* will be.)

If we could see Adam and Eve as they were in Eden, they would probably take our breath away. If they could look at us from the Garden and see us as we have become over the centuries —even the greatest athletes or the most popular movie stars—they would probably be shocked and feel sorry for us.

God will decide how our perfect bodies will look, and there is no reason to think we'll all look alike. Different heights and weights seem as likely as different skin colors. Maybe people who are tall now will have tall resurrection bodies; those who are short might remain short. Who knows? But we do know God is the Creator, the Artist, and the Inventor of variety. And we know all of us will be perfectly happy with the way God made us (just as we should try to be even now).

We won't be proud or stuck-up about how we look. But we'll never feel embarrassed either. We won't look into the mirror wishing for different hair, eyes, ears, or teeth. We won't have to work hard to look nice, because God will make us look fine and stay fine, maybe without our even trying.

Will we be able to fly and do other great stuff in our new bodies?

If you could have any ability (even that of a super-hero), what would you wish for? Some of you might want to fly like a bird, leap over a mountain, or fight like a ninja. (Or have the abilities of the Parr family in *The Incredibles*.)

When Jesus came back to life, he had a new body with some amazing abilities. He could appear to his disciples suddenly in a locked room (John 20:19). He was able to disappear from the sight of the two followers at Emmaus (Luke 24:31). When Jesus left the earth, he wasn't held down by gravity but went up into the air (Acts 1:9). That was called his ascension into Heaven. Amazing, huh?

It's possible that Jesus, who is both man and God, has certain physical abilities that we won't have. Appearing and disappearing could have been a way of showing that Jesus is everywhere. His ascension might have been something that only Jesus' body could do.

However, we're told in many passages in the Bible that our new bodies will be like his, so we may be able to move and travel in different ways than we can now. We don't know the amazing plans

God has for our bodies. We may be able to dive like a whale or fly like an eagle on the New Earth. Maybe we'll run like a cheetah or climb a mountain like a goat. (And who knows what cheetahs and goats may be able to do!)

How old will we be in Heaven?

Will a baby who dies be a baby forever in Heaven? Will the man who dies at ninety appear to be ninety as he walks on the New Earth?

People—grown-ups as well as kids—have always asked questions like these. Some believe that we'll all be the same age Jesus was when he died (about thirty-three). Others believe that we'll be the age we were when we died, except for older people. They would be the age they were when they stopped growing—before their bodies started to get older and weaker.

So you might think, *Hey, I'm a kid. Will kids who go to Heaven be kids once they get there, or not? Will there be any kids on the New Earth?* Isaiah 11:6, 8 describes an Earth where "the calf and the year-ling will be safe with the lion, and a little child will lead them all. . . . The baby will play safely near the hole of a cobra. Yes, a little child will put its hand in a nest of deadly snakes without harm."

Isaiah 11 may just be speaking of a thousand-year period on the old Earth called the Millennium. If Isaiah 11 is speaking of New Earth, it's possible that kids who die and go to Heaven might be allowed to grow up on the New Earth after Jesus returns—wouldn't that be a great neighborhood?! Christian parents might get to see their kids grow up. And if you had a brother or sister or friend who died, you, too, might get to enjoy their growing-up years on the New Earth.

On the other hand, it's possible that on New Earth we will appear ageless like the elves of Tolkien's *Lord of the Rings*. Maybe your parents and grandparents will always seem older to you than your little sister, but to their own parents and grandparents, they might seem young.

Since the Bible doesn't give any definite answers to this question about age, we'll just have to wait and see how old we look when we arrive in Heaven. Whatever the answer is, we know that we will look great and feel great, and we'll be excited about the resurrection bodies God gives us.

Will we wear clothes?

Clothes are important to us. What do you like to wear? Jeans? Shorts? Anything and everything as long as it's purple?

Because Adam and Eve were naked without being embarrassed before they disobeyed God, some people say we won't need to wear clothes in Heaven. Before you freak out, there's good news. Even prior to the final resurrection, which will happen at the time of Jesus' return to Earth, people are already described as wearing clothes—white robes that show purity, thanks to Jesus (Revelation 3:4; 6:11). Even the risen Jesus is described as wearing a robe in Heaven. So it appears we'll wear clothes—not because there will be shame or temptation, but maybe because they will improve our appearance and comfort.

Wearing robes might seem kind of funny to us, unless we're in a Christmas play. But to first-century people, anything *but* robes would seem strange, because that's what they wore most of the time. So that's probably what they'll wear in Heaven.

We can imagine ourselves dressed in Heaven the way people in our culture dress on Earth. Does that mean some people will wear jeans and T-shirts, while others will wear dressier clothes? Why not? Just as we wear different clothes for different occasions here, we may do the same on the New Earth.

White is the color most often associated with clothing in Heaven. The white clothes may show our status with God (Revelation 7:9), just as they showed Jesus' relationship to God during his experience on top of a mountain (Matthew 17). The emphasis on white may also relate to being clean.

Surprisingly, the only person described in Heaven as wearing a robe that isn't white is Jesus: "He wore a robe dipped in blood" (Revelation 19:13). This likely isn't actual blood but a red robe that's a symbol of Jesus' dying for all the bad things we've done.

Seven angels are described as wearing golden sashes (Revelation 15:6). Because many people from different countries wear colorful clothing, we should expect them to do this in Heaven, too. We'll talk more later about how resurrected people will keep their national heritages.

The book of Revelation tells us we'll be priests, kings, and queens in Heaven. God designed special clothes for the priests in Old Testament times (Exodus 28:3-43). So it's likely that as God's royal children we will wear a variety of beautiful clothes as we rule the earth under the direction of Jesus, the King of kings.

Will we eat and drink in Heaven?

Think about the food you most enjoy. Is it pizza? French fries? Chocolate cake? Mint-chocolate-chip or cookie-dough ice cream, or just plain vanilla? Maybe your idea of Heaven is eating that food for thousands of years.

Many people are afraid that in Heaven there will be no need to eat or drink. But think about this: After his resurrection, Jesus asked his disciples for some food and ate a piece of fish in front of them (Luke 24:41-43). He proved that resurrected people *can* and *do* eat real food. He could have decided not to eat. But the fact that he did eat says a lot about what his resurrection body was like.

Other Bible verses say that we'll eat at feasts with Jesus in an earthly kingdom. Jesus said to his disciples, "I will not drink wine again until the Kingdom of God has come" (Luke 22:18). Another time Jesus said, "Many Gentiles will come from all over the world—from east and west—and sit down

with Abraham, Isaac, and Jacob at the feast in the
Kingdom of Heaven" (Matthew 8:11).

An angel in Heaven said to John, "Blessed
are those who are invited to the wedding feast of
the Lamb" (Revelation 19:9). What do people do
at any meal or feast—especially a wedding meal?
Eat and drink, talk, tell stories, celebrate, laugh,
and have dessert. Wedding feasts in the Middle
East often lasted a full week. One day, while eating in the home of a Pharisee, Jesus said to his
host, "When you put on a luncheon or a banquet
. . . invite the poor, the crippled, the lame, and the
blind. Then at the resurrection of the righteous,
God will reward you for inviting those who could
not repay you" (Luke 14:12-14). After Jesus referred
to the resurrection of the dead, a man at the same
dinner said to him, "What a blessing it will be to
attend a banquet in the Kingdom of God" (Luke
14:15). If the man who said this had a wrong idea
about eating in Heaven, Jesus could have told him
so. But he didn't. In fact, he built on the man's words
to tell a story about someone who prepared a banquet and invited many guests (Luke 14:16-24).

So, will we eat and drink in Heaven? The
answer is a very clear *yes!*

Will we ever be tempted to do wrong things?

The fact that Adam and Eve—two people who lived in a perfect place—messed up causes many people to wonder if we'll mess up someday in Heaven. After all, Satan, a former angel, totally blew it with God. And didn't he live in Heaven when he first sinned?

Let's see what the Bible says. In Heaven "there will be no more death or sorrow or crying or pain. All these things are gone forever" (Revelation 21:4). The Bible also says that "the wages of sin is death" (Romans 6:23). Because sin always leads to death and sorrow and pain, the promise that there will be no death or sorrow or pain is also a promise that *there will be no sin.*

The Bible says that God *cannot* sin. It would be against his nature. Once we are with him in Heaven, it will be against our nature too. We won't want to sin any more than Jesus does—and he'll never want to do it at all.

Jesus said, "The Son of Man will send out his angels, and they will weed out of his kingdom *everything* that causes sin and *all* who do evil. They will throw them into the fiery furnace. . . . *Then* the righteous will shine like the sun in the kingdom of their Father" (Matthew 13:41-43, NIV, italics added).

What will be weeded out? *Everything* that causes sin and *all* who do evil. *Then* we will shine as brightly as the sun, just like Jesus. Sin will no longer be able to touch us.

Will we have the freedom to make our own choices?

God doesn't force us to obey him. He gives us the freedom to make that choice. *Free will* is the freedom to choose to obey God or disobey him. God won't take that freedom away from us in Heaven.

Having this free will might sound as if we'll be free to mess up in Heaven. However, as I mentioned in the answer to the previous question, we'll no longer *want* to do wrong things. Why? Because of Jesus. (Take a look at Romans 5:19.) The inability to sin doesn't mean we won't have free will. God *cannot* sin, yet no created being has greater freedom of choice than God the Creator.

Jesus died *once* to deal with sin and will never again need to die (1 Peter 3:18). Remember, Jesus promised to make all things new (Revelation 21:5).

We will be new people. Although we'll still be our old selves, we won't have the same old desires to do wrong.

We'll *never* forget how terrible it is to hurt God and others. People who've experienced severe burns aren't tempted to walk too close to a bonfire. Having known what life was like with its temptations on this earth, we who will experience new life in Heaven will never want to go back to that old life.

If the thought of sin ever came to us, we'd think, *Sin? Been there, done that. It was awful; only an idiot would choose that path.* The good news is, in Heaven we'll never be idiots! We'll never be tricked into thinking that God is holding back something good from us or that doing something sinful would be more fun and exciting.

In Narnia, Aslan comes to a world that is "always winter and never Christmas." When he arrives, the ice starts to melt, signaling a coming change to the whole land. The White Witch's sledge (a type of sled or horse-drawn sleigh) begins breaking through to warm mud.

"This is no thaw," said the queen's dwarf-driver, suddenly stopping. "This is Spring. What are we to do? Your winter has been destroyed, I tell you! This is Aslan's doing."

Just as Aslan came to save Narnia from the power of the White Witch, Jesus came to save Earth from Satan's power. The Bible tells us, "The Son of God appeared for this purpose, to destroy the works of the devil" (1 John 3:8, NASB).

Sin and Satan will *never* get hold of the earth or us again. Though we will have desire and free choice, not only will we never *want* to sin, we will never *want* to want to sin.

Will all people get the same rewards in Heaven?

We usually want to be treated the same as everyone else (unless everyone else is treated badly, of course). If your brother gets five Christmas gifts, you want five Christmas gifts, right? If your twin sister gets to stay up past her bedtime, you want to as well. When that doesn't happen, what do you do? Crab and complain?

In some ways, all people will be treated the same in Heaven. Jesus told a story about some workers who were hired at the beginning of a

day and those who were hired one hour before
quitting time (Matthew 20:1-16). All of the
workers received the same pay. But the workers hired earlier complained. They felt that they
should get more money because they worked
the longest. Jesus said if the one doing the
hiring wanted to pay some people more than
they deserved, that was up to him. No one else
had a right to complain. God's grace is often
surprising.

Jesus' story is a reminder that all people who
believe in him will wind up in the same place:
Heaven. This goes for the person who begins to
trust Jesus at the age of seven and someone who
doesn't trust Jesus until the age of ninety-two.
God will love everyone the same. However, they
won't all have the same rewards in Heaven.

Most Christians don't talk about rewards
very often, even though the Bible does. Maybe it's
because they are afraid people will seek rewards for
the wrong reasons. Or that they will brag about
their rewards in Heaven. But that's silly, because
none of us will brag in Heaven except about Jesus!
Here are just a few of the many important things
the Bible says about rewards in Heaven:

- "Remember that the Lord will reward each one of us for the good we do" (Ephesians 6:8).

- "God is not unjust. He will not forget how hard you have worked for him and how you have shown your love to him by caring for other believers" (Hebrews 6:10).

- [Jesus said,] "I tell you the truth, anyone who gives you a cup of water in my name because you belong to Christ will certainly not lose his reward" (Mark 9:41, NIV).

- "I am the one who searches out the thoughts and intentions of every person. And I will give to each of you whatever you deserve" (Revelation 2:23).

Some Bible verses mention that we'll have different rewards and positions in Heaven, according to the way we serve God now. For example, Jesus told a story about some servants who were rewarded in different ways for serving their master. (See Matthew 25:14-30.)

Jesus told another story that included these words: "'Well done!' the king exclaimed. 'You

are a good servant. You have been faithful with
the little I entrusted to you, so you will be gov-
ernor of ten cities as your reward'" (Luke 19:17).
Another servant was made leader of five cities.

Those who have served Jesus more faithfully
on Earth will receive greater reward and responsi-
bility on the New Earth. But in Heaven, we won't
complain or whine, "Hey, that's not fair!" We'll
know that all of God's choices for rewards are
right. And we'll never envy others or resent
them.

Because we know it's very important never
to believe we can do things to earn our way
to Heaven, we sometimes put down the idea
of doing good works to serve God. But the
Bible says that even though doing good works
can't earn our way to Heaven, those who are
going to Heaven should look for good works
to do that please God. In fact, the Bible says,
"We are God's workmanship, created in Christ
Jesus to do good works, which God prepared in
advance for us to do" (Ephesians 2:10, NIV).

Good works include helping and doing kind
things for people, such as visiting someone in a
nursing home, baking cookies for your neighbor,

or making hot chocolate for a family member. Other good works that God will reward if you have the right attitude: writing an encouraging note, saying thank you, helping Mom with the dishes, clearing the table, walking the dog.

Sharing Jesus with others, praying for people, letting other people borrow and use your things, and giving money to your church are all good works. God has made you to do good works, and he has planned for you to do them. So if you ask him what you can do for him and others, he'll show you. And he'll give you the strength to do these good things. I hope knowing this will encourage you to do some good works.

Will we know everything?

Maybe you're the smartest kid in your family or neighborhood or class. That means you know quite a few things. Still, the smartest person in the world knows only a tiny bit of *all* there is to know. Only God knows *everything*.

When we die and go to live with God, we'll certainly understand things more clearly, and we'll know much more than we do now. But even then we'll *never* know everything. Why? Because we're not God. Because we haven't been around since the beginning the way God has, and we are created beings, not the Creator.

The apostle Paul, a very smart man who wrote much of the New Testament, wrote this: "Now we see in a mirror, dimly, but then face to face. Now I know in part, but then I shall know just as I also am known" (1 Corinthians 13:12, NKJV). What he meant was that when we see God, we'll know a whole lot more about him and ourselves than we do now. And what we know will be correct. It will be true.

Even angels don't know everything. Just like us, though, they desire to know more (1 Peter 1:12).

If you read only part of a book or see part of a movie, you don't know the whole story, do you? It's only when you finish the book or see the movie credits roll that you know the whole story. That's how life is. We get only part of the story here on Earth. But God knows everything from start to finish. He knows everything that has ever happened and ever will happen. He knows every decision any person has ever made or ever will make.

There are some events we might not understand
on this earth. For example, we don't understand why
hurricanes happen or innocent people are killed.
Yet Paul wrote that "God causes everything to work
together for the good of those who love God and are
called according to his purpose for them" (Romans
8:28). How's that possible? Because God knows
everything. In Heaven we'll understand why certain
things happened and how God brought good even
out of painful times. (Including the painful times in
your own life.)

One day we'll see God and truly know him
(Revelation 22:4). Then things will make sense.
We'll never understand everything, but we'll know
and trust the God who does understand everything.
So we'll never again have reason to worry. (And if
we realize now that God is good and knows all and
can do whatever he wants, we don't have to worry
now either.)

Will we learn new things?

What would you like to learn to do? Water-ski?
Ride a horse? Paint? Speak Portuguese or Chinese?
Write a book?

I heard someone say, "There will be no more learning in Heaven." But according to God's Word, we will forever continue learning.

The Bible says, "God raised us up with Christ and seated us with him in the heavenly realms in Christ Jesus, in order that in the coming ages he might show the incomparable riches of his grace" (Ephesians 2:6-7, NIV). The word *show* means "to reveal." This means God will keep showing or revealing more things about himself so we can continue learning more about him.

Jesus told his disciples, "Let me teach you" (Matthew 11:29). In Heaven we'll have the privilege of listening to Jesus teach while we sit at his feet as Mary did (Luke 10:39). We'll also enjoy walking with him over the countryside, always learning from him, as his disciples did. Perhaps angel guardians or loved ones already in Heaven will be assigned to guide or tutor us. Maybe we'll even be allowed to tutor others who enter Heaven after we do!

There's so much to discover in this universe, but in our present lives here on Earth we have so little time and opportunity to learn all the things we want to learn. We'll have plenty of time in Heaven. Among

other things, we'll be able to explore the New Earth
and discover amazing things about God's creation, all
of which will tell us more about our Creator.

Will we sleep?

Like to sleep in on Saturdays and holidays? After a
hard week of school, maybe you enjoy sleeping late
as your reward for getting up early all week.

Our lives in Heaven will include rest. "Blessed
are those who die in the Lord from now on. Yes, says
the Spirit, they are blessed indeed, for they will rest
from their hard work" (Revelation 14:13).

What's your idea of rest? Silencing the alarm
on your radio/CD player/alarm clock? Lazing on
the couch in front of the TV? The Garden of Eden
provides a different definition of rest, one that
includes work that's meaningful and enjoyable, lots
of good food, a beautiful place to live, and nonstop
friendship with God, other people, and animals.
Even in the peaceful Garden of Eden, however, one
day was set aside for special rest and worship. (You
can read about it in Genesis 2:3.) This tells us that
while work will be fun on New Earth, we'll have
regular times of rest.

If our lives on New Earth will be so restful, will we need to sleep? Some people argue that sleep won't be necessary because we'll have perfect bodies. But the same argument would apply to eating—yet we *will* eat. Adam and Eve were created perfect, but did they sleep? Probably. God made us to need and enjoy sleep.

The Bible doesn't answer this question directly, so I'm guessing. But sleep is one of life's great pleasures. It's part of God's perfect plan for humans in bodies living on the earth. (Nightmares aren't, so we don't need to fear having those.) If we'll eat, walk, serve, work, laugh, and play in Heaven, why wouldn't we sleep?

Will we each have our own place to live?

Do you have your own room? If you share one with your brother or sister, maybe you can't wait for the time when you'll have a room of your own. Many Christians are counting on having their own place in Heaven.

Jesus said, "In my Father's house are many rooms. . . . I am going there to prepare a place for you" (John 14:2, NIV). *Place* is singular, but the word *rooms* is plural. This suggests Jesus has in mind for each of us an individual dwelling that's a smaller part of the larger place. This place will be the most special home we've ever had.

The term *room* is cozy and private. The term *house* suggests a large space shared with other people. That's Heaven: a place both huge and private. Some of us enjoy coziness, being alone in a quiet space. Others enjoy a large, wide-open space. Most of us enjoy both—and the New Earth will offer both.

Heaven isn't likely to have houses that are all the same. God loves being creative, doesn't he? Just look around, and you'll see what I mean. He makes things special for each of the children he loves. When we see the particular place he's prepared for us, whatever it is, my place will feel "just right" for me, and yours will feel "just right" for you. We'll be comfortable and perfectly happy because we'll be home!

If you feel at home in your house now, just wait until you live in the place Jesus is preparing for you on the New Earth!

Chapter 7

WHO WILL WE HANG OUT WITH IN HEAVEN?

We want you to know what will happen to the believers who

have died so you will not grieve like people who have no hope. . . .

First, the Christians who have died will rise from their graves.

Then, together with them, we who are still alive and remain

on the earth will be caught up in the clouds to meet the Lord

in the air. Then we will be with the Lord forever. So encourage

each other with these words.

1 THESSALONIANS 4:13, 16-18

"Welcome, in the Lion's name. Come further up and further in." Then Tirian saw King Peter and King Edmund and Queen Lucy rush forward to kneel down and greet the Mouse and they all cried out "Reepicheep!"...
Everyone ... seemed to be there. . . . Puddleglum the Marsh-wiggle ... Trumpkin the Dwarf... the two good Beavers and Tumnus the Faun. And there was greeting and kissing and handshaking and old jokes revived.

C. S. Lewis, *The Last Battle*

Will we just hang out with Jesus, or will we have other friends too?

Who are the people you hang out with most? Some people feel guilty because they want to spend more time with their friends than with God. (This is because they don't know much about God and how great it is to spend time with him!) If you've ever felt that way, there's good news: When you really get to know Jesus, you'll realize he is your very best friend!

But Jesus wants you to have other friends too. He values friendship and made all of us with a desire for relationships with other people. This started back in Genesis when God said, "It is not good for the man to be alone" (Genesis 2:18). The Bible also says, "Two people are better off than one, for they can help each other succeed" (Ecclesiastes 4:9). So God understands our need to have friends and our desire for those friendships to continue in Heaven. He's the one who made us that way! In Heaven we'll be able to have our same old friends—all those who know Jesus—and lots of new friends, too. A thousand years from now you will probably still be making brand-new friends. But because you'll have plenty of time, and money won't prevent you from traveling, you won't have to give up old friends to make new ones!

Has anyone close to you died? Do you look forward to being with that person in Heaven? Look at the great words from 1 Thessalonians 4 at the beginning of this chapter. God says that when Christians grieve it's different than when others grieve. Why? Because we know in Heaven we will be together again with those we love. We will be with the Lord forever, and with each other forever.

When a loved one who knows Jesus dies, of course it's still very hard for us. Jesus understands that—he himself cried after Lazarus died, because he didn't like death, and he knew Mary and Martha were terribly sad (John 11:35).

We should remind ourselves, however, that death isn't the end of our relationships. It's just an interruption. It's like the people who have died have gone on a trip ahead of us, but later we're going to join them. And then we'll always be together. So our separation from them isn't forever. It's only for a brief time.

When King Tirian walks into Heaven in *The Last Battle*, he suddenly feels a beard against his face and hears a voice he hasn't heard for many years: his father's. Their reunion is sweet and special. In fact, the reunion in Heaven shown in *The Last Battle* goes on and on, naming many of our favorite characters in Narnia. Don't you look forward to reunions like that? I sure do. I have a lot of friends and family who are with Jesus. And next to being with Jesus, I think the best thing about Heaven will be seeing my mom and dad and my friends Greg and Jerry and so many others.

I really mean it when I say the best part of Heaven will be hanging out with Jesus. I'm not just saying that because it's what I'm supposed to believe. It's what I really *do* believe. I became a Christian when I was in high school. Every year since then I've come to know Jesus better and love him more. There's no one like him. He's the best!

While Jesus was here on Earth, crowds followed

him because they loved him and wanted to be near him. He was more popular than an actor, a rock star, or a great athlete. But, unlike those people, he will never disappoint you or let you down. Being near Jesus is what will make Heaven what it is—Heaven! What could be better than that?

For those of us who know Jesus as the Son of God—our Savior—we can't help but look forward to being in the awesome crowds around him in Heaven. Jesus is the one who can change everything. His birth changed the way we keep track of time—the years before his birth are known as BC (before Christ). Even more important, he can change you as well—and he already has if you've let him. Jesus gives you peace and hope as you turn away from your sins and look forward to the life God has planned for you on this earth and the New Earth.

While Jesus will be our best friend, God the Father will be delighted to see us having other great friendships in Heaven too. I'm a father, and I can tell you that nothing makes a father happier than watching his children enjoy each other's company! God loves it when we have good friends now, and

in Heaven he'll provide us the best friendships
we've ever had.

Will there be families in Heaven?

How many people are in your family? What do
you love about being in your family? Just think:
Every member of your family who knows Jesus
will be part of your family forever. (If *you* know
Jesus, that is. Do you?) This is a great comfort to
all of us who have had one or more family members die.

Heaven won't be without families. In fact,
we'll all be part of one *big* family. We'll have family relationships with people who were related to us
on Earth (Aunt Chantel; Cousin Ezra). But we'll
also have family relationships with our friends, both
old and new. These relationships will be good, not
bitter or sad.

Maybe your family isn't perfect. (No one's is.)
If being with family members forever doesn't sound
too thrilling to you, remember in Heaven your
family—and you—*will* be perfect!

In Heaven nobody will bug us, and we'll never
bug anybody. Won't that be awesome? Our family

members will never cause us pain, and we'll never hurt them, on purpose or by accident. Our relationships will be what we've always wished—or should have wished—they would be.

When someone told Jesus that his mother and brothers wanted to see him, he answered, "My mother and my brothers are all those who hear God's word and obey it" (Luke 8:21). Jesus also said that those who follow him will gain "brothers, sisters, mothers, children" (Mark 10:30). I think of this whenever I meet a Christian and we experience a warm relationship right away.

Are there people you're not related to who are like a brother or sister or aunt or uncle or mom or dad to you? In Heaven we'll be one big happy family. But it'll be even better than now, because all our friends will also be family members, and all our family members will also be friends.

We'll all be happy to stay together in our heavenly family because of our common love for God, our heavenly Father, and his love for all of us. Every time we see another person, it will be like having a favorite family member come to visit!

Will people get married?

One of the religious leaders asked Jesus a trick question about marriage. Jesus answered, "When the dead rise, they will neither marry nor be given in marriage" (Matthew 22:30).

So Jesus' answer, recorded in the Bible, says that some things will be different on the New Earth. We will all be one big family, where marriage won't exist in the same way it does now. But the most important thing about a marriage is the special love and friendship that a husband and wife share with each other. That's a picture of the wonderful love and friendship that Jesus and all of the people who know him will share in Heaven.

When Paul talks about marriage he calls it "a great mystery, but it is an illustration of the way Christ and the church are one" (Ephesians 5:32). Jesus has proven forever how much he loves us, more than any husband has ever loved his wife. After all, he chose to die on the cross for us. How could we not return that love?

Although Jesus said people won't get married in Heaven, he never said that married people would stop loving each other. Remember, in Heaven we will be the same people (made better), with memories of our lives on Earth and the things we enjoyed with others. So those who had great times together and faced great difficulties together in this life will naturally have close relationships in Heaven.

My wife, Nanci, is my very best friend. Couples with good marriages usually are best friends. There's no reason to believe they won't still be best friends in Heaven.

· If your parents or aunt and uncle or other people you know are divorced, don't worry about whether they will get along with each other, or with you, in Heaven. Everyone who loves Jesus will be in Heaven, and everyone in Heaven will get along great with everyone else. Couples will be closer friends with some than with others, but there won't be anyone who doesn't like anyone else. No one will feel left out. Those kinds of problems will be left behind forever when we join Jesus in Heaven.

If some people we love go to Hell, won't we be sad in Heaven?

Have you ever heard someone ask, "If God is good, why do some people go to Hell?" The answer is that we are sinners and God is holy. Remember what I told you back in chapter six about free will? And how Jesus died so no one would have to go to Hell? Instead, people can go to Heaven forever if they confess their sins and trust Jesus to save them. But, sad to say, some people *have* died without choosing to follow Jesus. When someone rejects or refuses to follow Jesus, God's Son, that person also rejects God the Father (John 5:23; 15:23). And since Heaven is where God lives, to reject the true God is to reject Heaven.

Some people you know may choose not to believe in God or obey his teachings. Although God doesn't want anyone to do that, he doesn't force anyone to follow him. And since Heaven (which will become New Earth in the future) is the place where God lives, it is the home only of those who want to be there with him.

In Heaven we'll have a better understanding of what a fair judge God is. We'll know that every-thing he does is exactly right. (We can trust him even now, before we understand everything, believ-ing that he will always do what's right.) Someday we'll see clearly that God gave everyone a chance to know him (Romans 1:18–2:16).

We'll also understand the truth revealed in

2 Peter 3:9 (NIV): "The Lord is not slow in keeping his promise, as some understand slowness. He is patient with you, not wanting anyone to perish, but everyone to come to repentance."

We will marvel at the patience God showed everyone. We'll be amazed at how long he gave people an opportunity to follow him.

No one deserves Heaven. However, God loves us so much that he sent his only Son, Jesus, to die on the cross so that everyone could have an opportunity to go to Heaven (John 3:16).

Meanwhile, we can and should pray that our family members and friends will choose to follow Jesus and accept God's gift of a home with him in Heaven.

A year after I became a Christian, my mother came to Christ. But for many years my father didn't know Jesus. He didn't become a Christian until he was eighty-four years old. I was sad for him for many years, and then when he followed Christ I was so happy I could have shouted!

But I have friends whose loved ones died without Jesus. Sometimes it's hard for them, but God gives them comfort. And perhaps, just before these family members died, some of them might have turned to Jesus. As Jesus saved the thief on the cross just before he died, promising him paradise (Heaven), he can save all who, at the last moment before death, turn to him.

And we do know this for sure—any sorrows we have now will disappear forever on the New Earth, just as darkness disappears when the light is turned on. The Bible promises, "He will wipe away every tear from their eyes . . . neither shall there be mourning nor crying nor pain" (Revelation 21:4, ESV).

This is God's promise. You can count on it.

Will our enemies become our friends?

Ever had friends in one grade at school who became your enemies in another grade? You might not have understood why you were no longer friends or why they seemed to like their new friends better.

If you've become a Christian, maybe you wonder how you can "love your enemies" as Jesus tells us to do in Matthew 5:44. But God gives us the power to love even those who hurt us.

Let me tell you a story of what I mean. Ever heard of Corrie ten Boom? She and her family kept Jewish people safe from the Nazis during World War II by hiding them in her house in Holland. (Corrie wrote a book about her experience called *The Hiding Place*, and there's an old movie about it too.) Well, in 1944, the Ten Booms were caught and put in prison. Corrie's dad died there. Corrie and her sister, Betsie, were later placed in the Ravensbrück concentration camp. Betsie, like many others, died in that place.

Years later, Corrie met one of the guards from the prison camp. Many of the guards at Ravensbrück had been very cruel to the people in the camp. But this man was a Christian now. When he stretched out his hand to shake hers, at first Corrie couldn't shake hands with him. After all, this man had been an enemy. But God gave her the power to forgive him and shake his hand.

In Heaven, God will make up for the sad things that happen on Earth. Since no one will have a desire to hurt others, everyone will be a friend. That means we'll be friends even with those we weren't friends with on Earth.

I sort of said this before, but I'm going to say

it again a little differently, because some kids wonder about it a lot. We will still hang out with some people more than others. But there won't be anyone in Heaven who will hate us or even dislike us. Don't worry, because we'll never feel uncomfortable around anyone we bump into on the New Earth.

Will we be the same race or have the same national heritage we have now?

God has always been a God of variety. He created people of all races. As Peter once said, "I see very clearly that God shows no favoritism. In every nation he accepts those who fear him and do what is right" (Acts 10:34-35).

In the book of Revelation, John saw a huge group of people "from every tribe and language and people and nation" (Revelation 5:9).

Since you'll be the same person you are now, that means you'll have the same race and national heritage. For instance, if you're Swedish now, you'll be Swedish then. If your parents, grandparents, or ancestors from long ago came from Mexico, China, or Sudan, you'll still have that national heritage in your resurrection body.

How do we know this? Well, Jesus was Jewish, right? The Bible tells us that as a descendent coming from the family of David, he has the right to rule the earth from Jerusalem. This means that in his resurrection body he is still a descendant of David, still a member of the Jewish race. Since our new bodies will relate to our old bodies like his new body related to his old body, then we know we, too, will continue to be the same race we are now.

What's cool about Heaven is that everyone will be happy about each other's differences, not upset by them. There will be no racial prejudice in Heaven. No one will dislike a person whose family is from another part of the world, or whose hair or skin color is different.

Of course, God doesn't want us to wait until we get to Heaven for this to be true. His desire is for us to love all people of every race right now. God created everyone. If we stop to think about it, we'll realize that the human race is more beautiful because we're different in appearance and background. And remember, every human came from Adam and Eve, so we're *all* related anyway!

The Bible tells us that on the New Earth there

will be nations with their own leaders. Speaking of the New Jerusalem, God says, "The nations will walk by its light, and the kings of the earth will bring their splendor into it. On no day will its gates ever be shut. . . . The glory and honor of the nations will be brought into it" (Revelation 21:24-26, NIV).

The "wise men," kings of foreign nations, once came to the old Jerusalem seeking to worship the newborn Messiah, King Jesus. On the New Earth huge numbers of "wise men" will journey to the New Jerusalem. We will humbly bow before King Jesus, worshipping him as he sits on the throne. We will offer him the treasures of our nations, and he will be pleased to receive them. The King will gladly turn over the ruling of these nations to those who served him faithfully in this life.

God will reward us with leadership positions according to how faithful we've been in serving him here and now. Have you asked Jesus recently how you can serve him as you faithfully help the people in your life? Your family? Friends? Neighbors? Team members? Teachers? People at church?

Will we speak just one language, or more?

How many languages can you speak? Many people wonder whether there will be just one language in Heaven—a language we'll all speak and understand. Well, in the book of Revelation, we find this: "They cried out in a loud voice" (Revelation 7:10, NIV). This single "voice," not voices, suggests they probably spoke the same language.

Remember the story of the tower of Babel back in Genesis? (Check out Genesis 11.) The people spoke one language at the time and decided to build a city with a tower. Their thought was, "This will make us famous and keep us from being scattered all over the world" (Genesis 11:4). But because of their pride, God caused them to speak different languages. As a result, they scattered and formed their own nations.

Okay, you might wonder what was up with that. Why would God want them to scatter? Well, God sometimes acts in ways that keep us from doing dumb things. He knew that the people building the tower wanted to stay together—but not in order to worship him. Becoming a powerful group would eventually have led to their destruction.

Someday, though, God will do what the tower builders couldn't do. He'll build a city for his people and bring together all who live in it.

What *couldn't* the tower builders do? In Genesis 11, the people attempted to connect Earth to Heaven with their city, making Heaven one with Earth. What *can* God do, and what *will* he do? In Revelation 21, we're shown that God will bring Heaven down to Earth, making Earth one with Heaven.

God will probably restore to all of us a common language (perhaps the same as the language spoken in the Garden of Eden, which seems to have existed until Babel). Why? To make communication easy, not frustrating.

God knew that at the time of Babel, one common language would have made it possible for the people to do anything they wanted (Genesis 11:6). Because their hearts were evil, that was bad. In Heaven, however, everyone's heart will be filled with God's goodness. So we will want to do only what is for God's glory and our good. God will no longer need to protect us from ourselves. We will never join together to destroy or mistreat others. We'll only serve others in some way.

I think it's likely that we'll speak our current languages too. In *The Lord of the Rings*, the people of Middle-earth had a common language in addition to the language unique to their people group. That's also true in many places in the real world, including Kenya, where different tribes have their own languages but everyone talks to each other in the "trade language," called Swahili. This gives you an idea of what language in Heaven might be like.

Since we'll be smarter, learning new languages will be easy and enjoyable. Who knows, eventually we may speak dozens of languages, or even hundreds, so we can communicate with all of our new friends in Heaven. How exciting would that be?

Chapter 8

WILL ANIMALS LIVE ON THE NEW EARTH?

*Then I heard every creature in heaven and on earth
and under the earth and in the sea. They sang:
"Blessing and honor and glory and power belong to the one
sitting on the throne and to the Lamb forever and ever."*

REVELATION 5:13

*"Creatures, I give you yourselves," said the strong, happy voice
of Aslan. "I give to you for ever this land of Narnia. I give you
the woods, the fruits, the rivers. I give you the stars and I give
you myself. The Dumb Beasts whom I have not chosen are yours
also. Treat them gently and cherish them but do not go back to
their ways lest you cease to be Talking Beasts."*

C. S. LEWIS, *The Magician's Nephew*

What plans does God have for animals on the New Earth?

The Bible tells us that animals were a very important part of God's creation. "God made all sorts of wild animals, livestock, and small animals, each able to produce offspring of the same kind. And God saw that it was good" (Genesis 1:25).

The Bible also says, "The LORD God formed from the ground all the wild animals and all the birds of the sky. He brought them to the man to see what he would call them, and the man chose a name for each one" (Genesis 2:19). Only humans and animals were formed from the earth, which makes us special. Now, let's get it straight: Animals weren't created in God's image, and they aren't equal to humans in any way. But still, God created animals and cares about them, which means we should care about them too.

People and animals share something unique: We're living beings. The fact that God has a future plan for people and for the earth strongly suggests that he has a future plan for animals as well.

Some kids who have been bitten or hurt by animals are afraid of them—but on the New Earth, no animals will be dangerous, and we'll never be afraid. We'll love being around them, just like Adam and Eve did. Animals were important in Eden, when the earth was perfect. So they'll probably be important on the New Earth, where everything will once again be perfect.

Remember Elijah? He was taken up to Heaven in a chariot pulled by horses (2 Kings 2:11). We're told there are horses in Heaven (Revelation 6:2-8). In fact, there are enough horses for all who are in the vast armies of Heaven to ride (Revelation 19:14). There are also armies of angels currently riding horses on Earth, even though they're invisible to us (2 Kings 6:17).

No other animals are mentioned in Revelation, probably because they don't play a role in Christ's second coming. (An army that comes to save God's people rides horses, not squirrels, anteaters, or guinea pigs.) But isn't it likely that since there are so many horses in Heaven, there are all kinds of other animals too? Why *wouldn't* there be? Why would we expect horses to be the only animals in Heaven?

Some people think the horses in the present Heaven are just a picture from Earth of something else totally different. However, even those people have to admit that a New Earth wouldn't be complete without animals. Since we know resurrected people in real bodies will live there on real ground, with real trees and mountains and rivers, there's no reason why there won't be real animals, too. In a passage speaking of the New Earth, God says animals—wolf, lamb, and lion among them—will lie down in peace together (Isaiah 65:25). While some people think this refers only to a temporary kingdom that will last a thousand years, I think it refers also to the eternal New Earth.

Jesus proclaims from his throne on New Earth: "I am making all things new" (Revelation 21:5, ESV). Jesus is talking about making *old things* new, rather than just making *new things* (not that he *couldn't* make new things). He seems to be saying, "I'll take all I made the first time, including people, nature, animals, and the earth itself, and bring it back in a way that's new, fresh, and unable to be destroyed." I believe this suggests that God may remake certain animals that lived on the old Earth. Which brings me to the next question. . . .

Will we see our pets again on the New Earth?

Pets are great, aren't they? I've often thanked God for my golden retriever, Champ—my dog when I was growing up. I have lots of great memories of running and playing and hanging out with Champ. I especially remember the many times when he crawled into my sleeping bag as I lay in my backyard looking up at the stars.

You might really love animals. If you do, that's good. If you've ever had a pet that died (or several, or maybe lots, like thirty-seven gerbils), you're probably wondering if you'll see him or her again.

God, who created the animals, has touched many people's lives through them. It would be simple for him to re-create a pet in Heaven if he wants to. He's the *giver* of all good gifts, not the *taker* of them.

God loves to give good gifts to his children (Matthew 7:9-11). So if it would please you to have one or more of your pets with you on the New Earth, that may be a good enough reason for God to make it happen.

Aren't you glad you've had two hamsters, a rabbit, a calico cat, and a chocolate lab? That might

mean that you will be a pet owner on the New
Earth, too. Or if your family wasn't able to have
a pet, Heaven may be the place where you'll have
a pet for the first time, and all of your friends will
unselfishly share their pets with you.

The most important passage on this subject
may be Romans 8:18-22. (You can read it yourself.)
It says that "all creation" suffers because of human
sin and longs for the deliverance that will come
with our resurrection. It's like everything around
us is yearning to be made free from suffering. But
there is good news—nothing in creation will rot
or die after God raises us from the dead. And our
resurrection will apparently be the means by which
all creation will be restored to its former glory, and
go beyond it.

I think there's every reason to believe that "all
creation" that longs for deliverance includes the
animals. At the time when God's people are raised
from the dead, creation will experience what it longs
for. It will be "set free from its bondage to decay"
(Romans 8:21, esv).

Romans 8 hints that some of the animals that
lived and suffered and died on this old Earth will be
the same ones restored to life in God's earthly kingdom

that's to come. They suffered because of our sin, so their bodies will be freed when we receive our new bodies. They will then live in a world where they will never hurt each other or people or be hurt by anyone.

So here's the question: If any animals on this old Earth will experience life without suffering on the New Earth, won't some of those animals probably be our pets?

It seems to me God could do one of three things on the New Earth: (1) create entirely new animals; (2) bring back to life animals that have suffered in our present world, giving them new bodies that will last forever; (3) create some animals brand-new *and* bring back to life some old ones. Only God knows for sure what he plans to do. But Romans 8 leads me to believe that on the New Earth we will likely live again with some of the pets we have loved.

Will extinct animals live on the New Earth?

Ever wish you could see a dinosaur? Which kind would you most want to see? The brachiosaur? The T. rex? As part of his original perfect Earth, God created animals and plants, including those that are now extinct. I think that extinct animals and plants will be brought back to life. By resurrecting his original creation, God could show a complete victory over sin and death. It was after the first people sinned that the curse fell on the earth, eventually resulting in whole species of animals dying out. But remember, God promises, "No longer will there be a curse upon anything" (Revelation 22:3).

Romans tells us, "Since the creation of the world God's invisible qualities—his eternal power and divine nature—have been clearly seen, being understood from what has been made" (Romans 1:20, NIV). Animals were created for God's glory *and* to show us what God is like. What could speak more of his awesome power than a tyrannosaur?

When talking to Job, God pointed out how we can see his greatness in the giant land and sea creatures (Job 40–41). Why shouldn't all people have the opportunity to enjoy these great wonders of God on New Earth?

If you saw *Jurassic Park*, imagine all the awesome majesty of those huge creatures but without the fear of being crushed or eaten by one of them. Imagine riding an apatosaurus—or flying on the back of a pterodactyl. God created these animals,

and they were part of a world he called "very good."
So why wouldn't we expect God to include them
when he makes "everything new"?

Might some animals talk?

Have you read the stories by Beatrix Potter about
Peter Rabbit, Mr. Jeremy Fisher, and other animal
friends? How about *The Wind in the Willows* by
Kenneth Grahame or the Narnia books by C. S.
Lewis? If you love any of these stories, I bet you
wish that animals really could talk. (It's okay, you
can admit it.)

At least one animal talked in the Garden of
Eden—the serpent, who turned out to be Satan.
We're told that the serpent was "more crafty than
any of the wild animals the LORD God had made"
(Genesis 3:1, NIV). This means that other animals were also crafty. Notice Eve didn't say "Wow,
Adam! A *snake* just talked to me!" She didn't seem
surprised that a snake *could* talk. So it's possible that
other animals—at least some of the other crafty
ones—talked too.

Animals, as God originally created them, were
smart—probably smarter than we imagine. The

most intelligent animals we see around us can't be compared to the way animals were before the first sin. Why? Because the wrong choices that Adam and Eve made affected all of creation. If people will be smarter and have more abilities on New Earth, should it surprise us that animals might also be smarter and have more abilities there?

How exciting to discover for ourselves someday the unbelievable things God has planned for the New Earth! You might want to thank him right now for whatever plans he has for his animal kingdom.

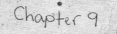

WHAT WILL WE DO
IN HEAVEN?

Blessed are the dead who die in the Lord from now on. . . . They
will rest from their labor, for their deeds will follow them.
. . . The throne of God and of the Lamb will be in the city,
and his servants will serve him.

REVELATION 14:13; 22:3, NIV

*There was the blue sky overhead, and grassy country spreading
as far as he could see in every direction. . . .*
*"It seems, then," said Tirian, smiling himself, "that the Stable
seen from within and the Stable seen from without are
two different places."*
"Yes," said the Lord Digory. "Its inside is bigger than its outside."
*"Yes," said Queen Lucy. "In our world too, a Stable once had
something inside it that was bigger than our whole world."*
*It was the first time she had spoken. . . . She was drinking every-
thing in even more deeply than the others. She had been
too happy to speak.*

C. S. Lewis, *The Last Battle*

Will Heaven ever be boring?

Many people think Heaven will be boring in a major
way. It's too bad, but some Christians also feel that
way.

People sometimes make fun of Heaven. They
say, "I'd rather be having a good time in Hell than
be bored in Heaven." Some imagine Hell as a
place where they'll hang around, shoot pool, and
joke with friends (like in Disney's *Pinocchio*). That
is *so* wrong. You could hang around with friends
and play and joke with them in *Heaven,* but not
in Hell. (Remember, Satan's a liar, and some of his
favorite lies are about Heaven and Hell.)

The fact is, Hell is a place where everyone is
lonely and miserable, where friendship and good
times don't exist. Hell will be deadly boring. Everything good, enjoyable, refreshing, fascinating, and
exciting comes from God. Without God—and all
the good things that come from him—there's nothing interesting to do. King David wrote, "You will
show me the way of life, granting me the joy of your
presence and the pleasures of living with you forever"
(Psalm 16:11). Just as without God there is *no* joy, so
in God's presence there's nothing *but* joy.

"Won't it be boring to be good all the time?"
someone asked. This guy believed that being bad
is exciting and being good is boring. But that's just
a big lie. (Don't fall for it, okay?) Doing wrong
things doesn't make life interesting; it makes life
complicated. Sin doesn't create adventure; it creates
emptiness. You may have guessed by now that my
favorite book series is The Chronicles of Narnia.
If you haven't read these books, I really encourage
you to. Aslan the lion is the king of the fictional
land Narnia just as Jesus is King of kings in the
real Kingdom of Heaven. So here's my question:
can you imagine *Aslan* ever being boring? Can

you imagine anyone hanging out with Aslan who isn't totally *excited* to be with him?

The stories tell us "Aslan is not a tame lion." He isn't under anybody's control. Like Aslan, the real Jesus is creative, fascinating, and *anything but boring*. You can be sure we will always wonder what more he has waiting for us. As our leader forever, he has plans that will just blow us away! I think Heaven is going to be full of great surprises and astonishing new adventures as we learn more about God and enjoy his wonders in a new universe.

Since Heaven is God's home, made by him, it will be awesome, satisfying, and interesting, just like God is. Once we're in Heaven, we'll think we were pretty dumb not to have looked forward to it more than we did. And we'll know without a doubt that there's no place we would rather be than with our Creator, God, who is powerful but who also loves us and really wants us to be there with him!

Will we *have* to work in Heaven?

Many people think of Heaven as a place filled with hammocks—one for each person to lie on and rest, rest, rest. Ever feel that way?

The truth is though we will rest, we will also *work* in Heaven. But just think: You won't have the "aw-do-I-have-to" feeling you might get when you're expected to do a chore now.

See, when Adam and Eve, the first people, broke God's law, work became difficult. God told Adam, "The ground is cursed because of you. All your life you will struggle to scratch a living from it. It will grow thorns and thistles for you, though you will eat of its grains" (Genesis 3:17-18).

On the New Earth we won't *have* to work. We will *want* to work. The work we do will be fun. Likewise, when it's time to rest, we'll want to rest. When it's time to gather and sing praises to our God, we'll want to do that. We'll always get to do what we want to do, and we'll always want to do what it's time to do.

We'll be able to do the work started by Adam and Eve: ruling over the earth for God's glory. We know this is true because we can read about it in the Bible. When a person enters Heaven after faith-fully serving God, he isn't offered the opportunity to stop working. Rather, he's told by his Lord, "Well done, my good and faithful servant. You have been faithful in handling this small amount, so now I will give you many more responsibilities. Let's celebrate together!" (Matthew 25:23).

Work in Heaven will never upset us or seem like a waste of time. Think about the kind of work you enjoy. When you're working on a hobby (painting, making things from wood, making jewelry, building models), work doesn't seem like work, does it? We're told that we will serve (work for) God in Heaven (Revelation 7:15; 22:3). We'll be just as excited to do our work in Heaven someday as we are to spend time on our favorite sport or hobby on Earth now.

Jesus told his disciples, "My nourishment comes from doing the will of God, who sent me, and from finishing his work" (John 4:34). Jesus found great satisfaction in his work. So will we!

Will we sing, dance, and make music?

What are your favorite tunes? Got an iPod attached to you? Music is an important part of life—something that many of us would be unhappy about leaving behind.

The good news is we *won't* leave it behind. There will be plenty of great music in Heaven.

The apostle John speaks of trumpets and harps in the present Heaven (Revelation 8:7-13; 15:2). If we'll have musical instruments right after we die and go to Heaven, it certainly seems that we can expect to find them on the New Earth after Jesus returns.

The Bible is full of examples of people praising God with singing and musical instruments. In the Temple, 288 people sang and played different instruments (1 Chronicles 25:1-8). The psalm writer instructed the people to praise God with trumpets, harps, lyres, tambourines, strings, flutes, and cymbals (Psalm 150). Hezekiah, one of the kings of Judah during Old Testament times, said, "I will sing his praises with instruments every day of my life in the Temple of the LORD" (Isaiah 38:20). Jesus sang with his disciples (Mark 14:26), and the apostle Paul instructed Christians to sing to the Lord (Ephesians 5:19).

We can expect some of the old songs written on this earth to be sung on the New Earth also. Revelation 15:2-3 describes people singing "the song of Moses"—probably the song of Exodus 15, where Moses and the people thanked God for rescuing them from Pharaoh and his army. (Perhaps we'll even sing Third Day songs. Who knows?) New songs will likely be written in Heaven too. Are you a songwriter? Maybe you'll write songs there.

Not only will there be singing, but there will be dancing as well! Not the kind of dancing that puts impure thoughts in our minds, but dancing that brings glory to God and is much more fun.

Throughout the ages, people have danced to God's glory on Earth (Ecclesiastes 3:4; Jeremiah 31:12-14). After the parting of the Red Sea, Miriam and the women of Israel danced and played tambourines, singing praises to God (Exodus 15:20-21). King David danced as he worshipped the Lord (2 Samuel 6:16). When the Prodigal Son returned home, the house was filled with music and dancing (Luke 15:25). Shouldn't we expect to dance in Heaven, too?

It's God who created us with the ability to dance. Just as we can use our voices and musical instruments as a way to worship God, so we can use dancing to honor him.

Will we laugh?

Like to laugh? Believe it or not, so does God.

Where did humor come from? Not from

people, angels, or Satan. God created all good things, including good humor. If God didn't have a sense of humor, we wouldn't either. That he has a sense of humor is very clear. Think about aardvarks and baboons. Take a good look at a giraffe, or your cat chasing a ball. You have to smile, don't you?

In Heaven, I think Jesus will laugh with us. In fact, his fun-loving nature will probably be our greatest source of endless laughter.

Am I just guessing about laughter? No. Jesus said, "God blesses you who weep now, for in due time you will laugh" (Luke 6:21). Did you hear that? *You will laugh.*

Jesus promises laughter as a reward in Heaven. As we look forward to the laughter to come, Jesus says we should "leap for joy" (Luke 6:23) now. Can you imagine someone leaping for joy in silence, without laughter? Take any group of people who are enjoying some kind of celebration (a birthday, a graduation, a family reunion, a church picnic), and what do you hear? Laughter. There may be hugging, playful wrestling, singing, and storytelling. But always there is laughter.

When life is hard, remember what Jesus promised about life in Heaven: "You will laugh."

Will we play?

Quick! What's the first thing you do when you have a free moment (after homework, chores, etc.)? You probably grab some playtime, right? Maybe you head outside to skate, shoot hoops, or ride your bike.

You don't ever have to be told to play your favorite game. If you have the time, you just do it, right? Does that please God? As long as it's not something that dishonors him—involving the occult or witchcraft or anything else immoral— God is happy for us to play. Of course, we can't just play all the time, but God does want us to have fun. After all, he invented fun, and he created us to enjoy fun.

Well, guess what? The fun doesn't stop on the old Earth. You'll have time to play on the New Earth. In fact, everyone who enters Heaven will need to be like a kid who loves and trusts God and who likes to have fun (Mark 10:14-15).

Someone once asked me: "Will there be toys in Heaven?" I believe the answer is yes. After all, we'll still be human, so why wouldn't we like toys? And we'll still have the ability to make things, so why not toys?

Do you wonder if God himself has a playful side? God says he has revealed what he's like in what he has created. (Remember Romans 1:20 from our discussion about extinct animals?) Think about things in nature that reveal God's playfulness—monkeys, kittens, dogs, horses, and lots of other animals.

Have you ever watched otters? I have. It's really fun. They'll spend almost the whole day sliding and splashing and playing and just having a blast! They were making water slides thousands of years before people did. And who built that into their nature? I'll bet you know.

You didn't think it was human beings who invented play and fun and joy, did you?

Will there be sports?

What's your favorite sport? Have you ever thought that you might enjoy that sport again someday after the resurrection, when you live on the New Earth, with a perfectly healthy body?

God compares the Christian life to sports competitions (1 Corinthians 9:24, 27; 2 Timothy 2:5). Sports and our enjoyment of them are a good thing. If people hadn't become sinners, they would

still have invented baseball and soccer and football
and basketball and competition swimming and div-
ing, don't you think? Sure! There would probably
be more and even better sports than there are today.

Who made us so we could invent games and
enjoy playing them? Satan? Of course not. Satan
can't create anything, and he's certainly not playful.
God made us. And sports are just a way to show
how he made us.

Ever see that 1981 movie *Chariots of Fire*?
It's one of my favorite movies ever, and yes, you
can still rent it. (They actually made movies long
before 1981!) The hero of that movie, Olympic
champion Eric Liddell of Scotland, was a real person who understood that glorifying God applies to
every part of our lives, including sports. Explain-
ing why he believed God had called him not only
to missions work in China but also to compete in
the Olympics, Liddell said to his sister, "He made
me fast. And when I run I feel God's pleasure.
. . . To give up running would be to hold him in
contempt." In other words, Eric felt he would not
show respect for God if he didn't use the ability to
run that God had given him.

In a tennis tournament, I once played a five-hour singles match in which each of the three sets went to a tiebreaker. I was exhausted; I had lost a couple of toenails; and I limped for two weeks afterward. But did I regret a single minute of that five-hour match? No way! There's joy in working hard when you're competing in a sports activity, isn't there? Those five hours started a friendship with the guy I played against. What great memories we both have of that match! And God, who made my mind and body, was right there with me the whole time.

What kinds of new sports activities might we play on the New Earth? The possibilities are limitless. Perhaps we'll play sports that were once too risky. Imagine snowboarding down the slopes of a newly shaped Mount Everest! Maybe you'll be able to play golf, baseball, soccer, tennis, hockey, football, or basketball with your favorite Christian athlete.

People have told me, "But there can't be sports in Heaven because competition brings out the worst in people." I help coach high school tennis, so I've seen my share of bad attitudes. But I've also seen very good attitudes. (And I've coached some Christian kids who have been great representatives of

Jesus.) I've also spoken at a number of NFL chapels
and have met quite a few pro football players who
really love Jesus and who play the game for God's
glory. It's true that some people behave badly while
playing sports. But it doesn't have to be that way.
And on the New Earth, sports will never bring out
the worst in us, because *there will be no worst in us
to bring out.*

Others say, "In sports, someone has to lose. And
in Heaven no one could lose." Who says so? I've
thoroughly enjoyed many tennis matches and ten-
kilometer races that I've lost. (In fact, I lost every one
of those races—by a long shot.) Losing doesn't have
to ruin your day, you know, not even here and now.
And it certainly *never* will in Heaven!

Think of what it will mean for people who've
never been able to walk. (That includes some of
you reading this book.) If you've always wished you
could run the bases and hit a home run or kick a
football, I think you'll get to do that. In fact, I can't
find a single good reason to believe sports won't be
part of our lives on the New Earth. I expect to see
most of the activities we enjoy now, with many new
ones we haven't thought of.

Think about this: Your favorite sport on the

New Earth may be one you've never heard of . . . or that hasn't even been invented yet! I have grand-children named Jake, Matthew, and Tyler. One day they may be inventors of those unbelievably popular New Earth sports called *Jake-ball*, *Matthew-ball*, *and Tyler-ball*!

Will there be art and entertainment?

Do you like a good movie or play? Maybe you enjoy painting or drawing. Believe it or not, God invented art. He created the universe, then wrote, directed, and took the leading role in history's greatest story. (It's called the Drama of Redemption.) He is the one who gives artists and writers the kinds of minds and emotions and physical senses that give them their ideas.

Will we find ways to use the arts—including drama, painting, sculpture, and music—to praise God? Will these arts continue to provide enjoyment and entertainment for people? I believe the answer is yes.

Think of the joy you feel when you make a card for your mom or grandpa, or when you draw a cartoon just to make your brother Zachary smile.

Or consider how you might feel if you and your cousins Ainsley and Hudson wrote and performed a skit at a family reunion. Then think about how awesome it would be to create something even better on the New Earth. Maybe a great play written by Savannah, starring her sisters Ellie and Julia and her cousins Bailey, Sawyer, and Sydney.

If we believe New Earth (Heaven) will be greater than our present Earth, then surely the greatest books, dramas, and poems are yet to be written. Authors will have new ideas and better ways of thinking. Awesome books, including exciting adventure stories, are just waiting to be written by Courtney and Camber. (And people will be eager to read them.) Mckinzie might paint beautiful landscapes. Christian might make sculptures, and Elena might fashion beautiful jewelry. Alexis and Spencer might compose and perform great songs, and maybe Logan will be the featured drummer.

I look forward to reading and perhaps writing books that describe how wonderful God is, helping me worship him better. And I'm eager to read about adventures you and others will be enjoying throughout the New Universe. I'd also like to see your plays and paintings of those adventures.

Okay, now you try it: "I can't wait to be part of making a _____ (fill it in) to be painted/presented/produced/performed by _____ (insert your name and some family members' or friends' names), all to the glory of the most important person in the audience: King Jesus Christ of Nazareth!"

Will there be stores and other businesses in Heaven?

Why do people create and run stores and other businesses? "To make money," you might say. Well, that's true. But that's not the only reason, is it?

Doesn't the manager of the hardware store enjoy helping people find just the right tools for their jobs? Doesn't the farmer enjoy growing things and making them available to others? Doesn't the master chef love to cook, and wouldn't he still love it if he didn't need the money? Doesn't the guy who fixes computers love to solve problems and have people say, "Thank you"? Doesn't the florist like to work with flowers and arrange them so they're really beautiful? Doesn't the lady who builds custom furniture love to see the look of wonder on people's faces as they run their hands over what she's made, even if they can't afford to buy it?

The first person Scripture describes as "filled with the Spirit" wasn't a prophet or priest; he was an artist and craftsman (Exodus 31:1-6). God created us to do things and to help or bring pleasure to other people by doing those things.

I'm a writer. I hope I help people with what I write. I know I love to give away my books. The truth is, I would gladly write books even if I were never paid a dime for it. (Don't tell that to the people who published this book!)

My wife and I have had the opportunity to give our time and money to others. And we've also received generous gifts from many people over the years. Giving and receiving go together. Both are really fun.

Most people think there will be no stores or businesses or trades in Heaven because no one will need to make money. But isn't it God who gives us the skills to create goods and services that are helpful to others? Won't he still want us to help people out in the New Earth society even though no one will need money?

I believe we may see people doing business on

the New Earth, but with a different twist. Money won't have anything to do with it. Not because making money is bad (it isn't), but because our needs will be met without money. I think we'll still be able to benefit from other people's creative work, and from the goods they produce or the services they offer.

You could say we won't *need* homes, food, and drink any more than we'll need goods and services, but won't we *enjoy* them anyway?

I can picture, on the New Earth, an artist creating a beautiful painting or sculpture or piece of jewelry and simply giving it away to provide pleasure for someone. Jesus freely gave his life away for others, and we'll be like Jesus in Heaven when it comes to giving.

Jesus, the greatest giver in the universe, said to us, "It is more blessed to give than to receive" (Acts 20:35). The word *blessed* includes the meaning of "happy-making." So the happiness in giving others what you've made, or giving them your time and help, goes beyond the joy of receiving. (When you *give* something you worked hard to make or find, like at Christmas, that's often more fun than receiving, isn't it?) So imagine stores where money isn't exchanged and anyone is welcome to come in and look over what's there. If a person likes a sweater, the owner could say, "Please, take it with you. God gave me the ability to make it, and I enjoyed doing it. I'd love to share it with you."

Maybe the person who takes the sweater wants to leave behind something from her garden, or a book or a picture frame or a baseball mitt . . . who knows? We'll do everything for God's glory and each other's good—and nothing will make us happier. All of it will deepen our friendships with people and with God.

Businesses and other occupations are important to God. While God loves to see his children doing work that helps others, God's Word tells us, "Work willingly at whatever you do, as though you were working for the Lord rather than for people" (Colossians 3:23). God certainly doesn't need anything from us, but he is pleased when we use our abilities to serve him. Just as we work for God on the present Earth, we will work for him on the New Earth. And we will love every single minute of it!

Will there be computers or other technology?

Would Heaven be Heaven without computers or cell phones? Sure it would. But does that mean they won't be there? We don't know for sure, but we do know that God isn't against technology. After all, God gave us the creativity to make it, and technology helps us rule the earth as he commanded.

God created a certain order to the universe and gave us minds to be able to figure out how to make things better. So what should we expect to find on New Earth? Earth stuff: tables, chairs, cabinets, wagons, machinery, transportation, sports equipment, and . . . technology.

Will there be new inventions or new twists on old inventions? Why not? The God who gave people the ability to create surely won't take that gift back (Romans 11:29).

When God gave the Garden of Eden to Adam and Eve, he expected them to do great things, like grow food and care for trees, other plants, and animals. That's what we're to do, too. Sometimes people fail to do what God wants. But on the New Earth, we'll totally succeed at doing everything God wants us to do.

A lot of our inventions help make life easier. Think of dishwashers, microwaves, and computers. But on the New Earth, we probably won't have to continually look for ways to make life easy. Maybe we'll just enjoy experimenting. (Don't you like to experiment?)

If people had never sinned, would we still have invented the wheel and created machinery? Would technology have developed? Certainly. On the New Earth, shouldn't we expect to come up with all kinds of inventions for the good of people and to show the greatness of our Creator, God?

Think about it—what kind of far-out inventions can you imagine? Maybe God will put you on the design team that comes up with them, or on the production team that builds them. Wouldn't that be exciting? And picture in your mind Jesus looking at what you've done, smiling, and saying to you, "Well done!"

Could it get any better than that?

What will travel be like?

In Narnia, Peter, Susan, Edmund, and Lucy travel by foot, horse, and sledge [sled]. But they first

arrive in Narnia by walking through the back of
a wardrobe. (That's a tall piece of furniture with
doors, and it's used as a closet.) In Oz, Dorothy
uses her feet and occasionally an animal, like a flying monkey. When she returns to Kansas, the silver
shoes (ruby slippers in the movie) help her travel.
In Middle-earth, people travel by foot, horse, ship,
or fell beast (if they are ringwraiths).

How do you like to travel? Plane? Scooter?
Skateboard? Bike? Your feet? You may be wondering if you will travel in any of your favorite ways on
New Earth. You may also be wondering whether
you will be able to appear suddenly in thin air, as
Jesus was able to do in his resurrected body (John
20:24-26). Might you be able to go somewhere
simply by thinking about it or wishing for it? Perhaps, but it's also possible that although our bodies
will be like Jesus' body, his ability to appear, disappear, and rise in the air is due to the fact that he's
God. We can't be sure, but we'll find out!

If there will only be small paths on the New
Earth, we might assume that walking will be the
only way to travel. But we're told the New Jerusalem
will have streets and gates. That suggests at least the

use of wagons or horse-drawn carts, or something more advanced, whether cars or something beyond.

Will we ride bicycles? Have flying machines? Will we travel to other places outside New Jerusalem in airplanes? We don't know. I think we should use the "why not?" test. The best reason for something not to be on the New Earth is that it's evil. Well, is there anything evil about wheels or motors or bikes or cars or airplanes? The answer is definitely no. Therefore, there's no compelling reason to believe we won't enjoy these kinds of travel on New Earth—or other higher-tech methods of transportation that haven't even been invented yet.

Remember, the New Earth won't be a complete return to the Garden of Eden, requiring us to give up such things as inventions, transportation, and technology. It'll be a renewed Earth with people who have better brains, capable of designing and building better machines. Imagine brilliant scientists and technicians with minds and bodies the way they were before the first people sinned— and even better. These are people who will never die and who will work together happily in complete cooperation. Wow! It might not be long before the space shuttle seems pretty old-fashioned!

Will we explore the universe?

God promises to make not only a New Earth but also "new heavens" (2 Peter 3:13). The "new heavens" refers to everything in the sky (what we can see and beyond—the entire universe).

Since God will bring back the old Earth and the old Jerusalem, changing both into Version 2.0, he can also change galaxies, stars, planets, and moons.

As a twelve-year-old, I first viewed through a telescope the great galaxy of Andromeda. It consists of hundreds of billions of stars and probably way too many planets to count. It's nearly three million light years from Earth. (Ask your parents if you can look at pictures of it on the Internet. It's very cool. It can even be seen with your eyes alone if you know exactly where to look.)

As I looked through that telescope, I was in awe of this galaxy. But I knew nothing about God, and I felt very small and alone. Years later I heard the gospel story of Jesus. After I became a Christian, I found that gazing through the telescope changed for me. It became an act of worship. It felt great that I knew the God who made this incredible universe.

Since the Andromeda Galaxy is part of this

creation, the Bible's promise of new heavens suggests there will be a New Andromeda Galaxy. From the night when I first saw that place as a fuzzy blur in my telescope, I've wanted to go there. I now think it's possible that one day I will.

God made billions of galaxies containing perhaps trillions of stars, planets, and moons. Not many people have seen more than a few thousand stars, and those have only been seen as dots in the sky. The heavens point to God's glory now, and we know we will be praising God forever. So don't you think our exploring the new heavens, and ruling over them, will likely be part of God's plan?

Many of us have enjoyed the pleasure of traveling on this earth. People journey across oceans and to outer space because God made us with the desire to explore and the creativity to make that desire a reality.

What will it be like to travel both the New Earth and the New Universe? Maybe you've read about people—especially astronauts—who have taken amazing journeys and wished you could do the same. In the New Universe, I think it's very likely you will.

By the way, I hope that when you study science,

it helps you see how creative and wonderful God is. Sure, the scientists who say there is no God are totally wrong. But many scientists realize that this amazing universe provides proof of how great our Creator is. I know that on the New Earth you'll love studying God's universe to learn more about him. Why not start now?

Will there be aliens on other planets?

The question of whether or not there are aliens on other planets has been discussed for centuries. No Bible passage proves either that God has or has not, or will or will not create other races of intelligent beings. Certainly he could do that, either on Earth or on other planets spread across the New Universe.

God has already created several kinds of intelligent beings, including angels and humans. The "living beings" who worship God in Heaven are clearly different than most of the angels (Revelation 4:6-11). And, as we have seen, there were "crafty" animals in the Garden of Eden, suggesting a high level of intelligence.

The Bible is clear that there will be "new heavens," meaning a new universe of stars and planets. It's possible God will put intelligent creatures on

them. God is the Creator. He'll never stop being
what he is. In the world to come, we should
expect new and surprising creations that honor
him, because God never runs out of ways to create
things. And let's face it, he enjoys making life.

Some people may say, "To imagine that God
will populate worlds with new beings is just science
fiction." We may have it backward. Writers create
science fiction and readers like it because God has
put within us a sense of adventure, wonder, and
imagination. Since God has a track record of creating intelligent creatures, it's not science fiction to
suggest he may do so again in the New Universe.

Like everything else that sinful humans do,
some science fiction stories are based on false ideas
that remove God from the picture. But this shouldn't
cause us to look away from all the ideas in science fiction of what a new universe might be like. We know
that our creative God will form the New Universe.
(It won't happen by a gradual process of evolution.)
Is God's imagination less than that of his people? Of
course not! He will do whatever he pleases and create
whatever he pleases in the ages to come. He'll just do
it, and we'll be happy—*really* happy—with whatever
he chooses to do.

Will we travel through time?

Because God is not limited by time, he may choose to show us past events as if they were happening right now. We may be able to study history from a front-row seat. Perhaps we'll have a chance to see the lives of our grandparents, and their parents and grandparents, as they lived on this present Earth. We may be able to watch our favorite Bible characters in action—for real, not just in a movie or a play.

Or maybe we'll see how our small acts of faithfulness and obedience changed the lives of others. Perhaps we'll see how we helped people become interested in following Christ. (Fortunately, we still have time to make a difference in people's lives, a difference that they—and we—will be grateful for later!)

Does the idea of time travel seem too strange to be a real possibility on New Earth? Think about it some more. If God would not be able to let us see the past, he wouldn't be God. So the question is this: Would he have good reasons for doing so? One reason might be to show us how he helped us and watched over us on this earth. Wouldn't that reveal to us God's greatness and give him glory?

Our God is called the one "who is able,

through his mighty power at work within us, to accomplish infinitely more than we might ask or think" (Ephesians 3:20). That means there is *no end* to how much more God can do than we could ever expect. Wow!

Knowing God, and how amazing he is, we can be sure of this much: Whatever is ahead of us, in the new heavens and on the New Earth, it's far better than you or I can imagine.

Chapter 10

HOW CAN WE KNOW WE'RE GOING TO HEAVEN?

I have written this to you who believe in the name of the Son of God, so that you may know you have eternal life.

1 JOHN 5:13

"Oh, Aslan," said Lucy. "Will you tell us how to get into
your country from our world?"
"I shall be telling you all the time," said Aslan. "But I will not
tell you how long or short the way will be; only that it lies across
a river. But do not fear that, for I am the great Bridge Builder.
And now come; I will open the door in the sky and send you to
your own land."...
"Are—are you there too, Sir?" said Edmund.
"I am," said Aslan. "But there I have another name. You must
learn to know me by that name."

C. S. LEWIS, *The Voyage of the Dawn Treader*

An eleven-year-old American girl wrote to C. S.
Lewis in England to find out Aslan's real name on
Earth. Lewis wrote back to her and asked:

> As to Aslan's other name, well I want you to
> guess. Has there never been anyone in this
> world who (1) arrived at the same time as
> Father Christmas; (2) said he was the son of
> the great Emperor; (3) gave himself up for
> someone else's fault to be jeered at and killed
> by wicked people; (4) came to life again; (5) is
> sometimes spoken of as a Lamb. . . . Don't you
> really know His name in this world? Think it
> over and let me know your answer! (*C. S. Lewis
> Letters to Children*, Lyle W. Dorsett and Mar-
> jorie Lamp Mead, Editors)

You know who Aslan really is, don't you? Besides knowing Jesus' name, though, have you come to know him as your Savior and Lord and best friend?

Jesus said, "I am the way, the truth, and the life. No one can come to the Father except through me" (John 14:6).

In Bible times each city kept a list of everyone who lived there. Guards were posted at the city gates to keep out criminals and enemies by checking their names against the list. God's Word explains how Heaven will be like those cities: "Nothing impure will ever enter [the city], nor will anyone who does what is shameful or deceitful, but only those whose names are written in the Lamb's book of life" (Revelation 21:27, NIV).

Jesus is called the Lamb, because lambs were sacrificed as offerings to pay the penalty for sins. As the Lamb of God, Jesus died for the sins of the world (John 1:29). And he has the "book of life," which is full of the names of all those who are his followers and will live with him in Heaven forever.

The Wedding Singer and the Book

A few years ago something unusual happened to
a professional singer I know, named Ruthanna.
Her story helps us understand how important it
is to have our names written in the Lamb's Book
of Life.

Ruthanna and her husband were excited because
she had been asked to sing at the wedding of a very
rich man. The party after the wedding was held on
the top two floors of the tallest skyscraper in Seattle.
Waiters in tuxedos passed out wonderful food and
drinks. The bride and groom cut a ribbon at the bot-
tom of the stairs that led up to the top floor. Then
they went up the stairs, and their guests followed.

At the top of the stairs stood a man with a big
book open in front of him. He spoke with everyone who was about to go through the door. To each
person he said, "May I have your name, please?" He
would check his book and make sure the name was
there before letting anyone in to the party.

When Ruthanna and her husband came to the
door, she gave the man their names. "I am Ruthanna
Metzgar and this is my husband, Roy."

He searched the names starting with the letter
M. "I'm not finding it. Would you spell it, please?"

Ruthanna spelled her name slowly. After searching the book, the man said, "I'm sorry, but your name isn't here."

"There must be some mistake," Ruthanna replied. "I'm the singer. I sang for this wedding!"

The man answered, "It doesn't matter who you are or what you did. Without your name in the book, you can't come to the party."

He motioned to a waiter and said, "Show these people to the service elevator, please."

The Metzgars followed the waiter past beautifully decorated tables covered with food that looked really good. The other room was filling up with well-dressed people who were having the time of their lives.

The waiter led Ruthanna and Roy to the service elevator, ushered them in, and pushed *G* for the parking garage. They found their car. Quietly and sadly, they drove away. After a while Ruthanna's husband asked her what had happened.

"When the invitation arrived, I was busy," Ruthanna replied. "I never bothered to send the note back telling them I was coming. Besides, I

was the singer. I thought I didn't have to respond
to the invitation to go to the party."

Ruthanna started to cry. It was partly because
she had missed the most amazing dinner party
she'd ever had a chance to attend. But it was partly
because she now had a little idea of what it will be
like someday for people who stand before Christ
and find their names are not written in the Lamb's
Book of Life.

Christ's invitation to his party is recorded in
the last chapter of the Bible: "Whoever is thirsty,
let him come; and whoever wishes, let him take
the free gift of the water of life" (Revelation
22:17, NIV).

Many people have been too busy to respond
to Christ's invitation to his party. Some think they
will get into Heaven to attend the greatest party
ever just because they have tried to do good things,
like going to church, being baptized, or helping
with little kids.

But people who do not say yes to Christ's invitation to forgive their sins are people whose names
aren't written in the Lamb's Book of Life. And if
you aren't allowed into Heaven's wedding banquet,

the only other place to go won't be a garage. It will be Hell.

There won't be any excuse for saying no to Jesus that will be good enough. If our names aren't written in the book, we'll be turned away.

Have you said yes to Christ's invitation to join him at his wedding feast? Have you asked Jesus to forgive your sins so you can spend eternity with him in his house? If so, you have reason to be happy— Heaven's gates will open wide for you.

If you have been putting off your response to Jesus, now would be a good time to put your trust in him and say yes to his invitation!

A Summary of the Gospel

When your parents want to take you to a place they've never been before, what do they do? They ask for directions from someone who knows where the place is, check a map, or use MapQuest. You'd better hope they *don't* just make a guess!

Wanna be sure you're going to Heaven? Let these verses from the Bible's book of Romans be your guide:

1. For everyone has sinned; we all fall short of God's glorious standard (Romans 3:23).

> Back in chapter one I answered the question, "If we're good, does that mean we'll go to Heaven someday?" In my answer I said that all of us have messed up or done wrong things. We may say, "But I didn't mean to!" or just call them failures or mistakes or "my bads." But the Bible calls them by a three-letter word: sin. To sin means to break *any* of God's rules against lying, cheating, stealing, or anything else. God is the only perfect model for us to follow, and he never sins. That means we can never come near his wonderful, glorious standard—not on our own, that is. However, God not only sets the standard but also provides a way for us to meet his standard. Read on. (Warning: The news gets worse before it gets better. But if you read it all, it will make sense, and it should make you happy.)

2. For the wages of sin is death, but the free gift of God is eternal life through Christ Jesus our Lord (Romans 6:23).

> Everyone receives a payment for sin. It's a salary that we earn, but it's *not* something we might look forward to, like cash or a check. Because Adam and Eve chose to follow Satan's advice in the Garden of Eden (Genesis 3), all people are born with the desire to go

their own way instead of God's. This means we are sinners, and the result of our sin is *death*. Spiritual death is separation from God in a very real place called Hell.

That's the bad news. The good news is that God has a free gift waiting for us. That free gift is just the opposite of the wages that our sins have earned. It's a gift that will last forever: *eternal life*.

You've been reading about eternal life all through this book. Right after death, God's people will enjoy life in the present Heaven. That will be followed by Christ's return and eventually life on the New Earth, where God will dwell with us forever. New Earth will be at the center of the eternal Heaven. This never-ending life will be fun, exciting, thrilling, and more amazing than anything you've ever experienced. To see God and worship him and walk the New Earth with Jesus and the people we love . . . wow!

Why does God offer such an unbelievable gift? Keep on reading. (From now on, the news just gets better and better.)

3. God showed his great love for us by sending Christ to die for us while we were still sinners (Romans 5:8).

God created people because he is a God of love, and he wanted us to love him back. But the bad things we think and do separate us from God. Because we all have blown it, we cannot get into Heaven as we are. All along, though, God had a plan to help us. He sent his Son, Jesus, to die for us. Jesus, who never did anything wrong, was the perfect choice.

When he was crucified (nailed to a cross to die), Jesus took upon himself a punishment *he* didn't deserve so we could live forever in the Heaven *we* don't deserve. Our ticket to Heaven is just as free as the one Aslan offered Edmund in *The Lion, the Witch and the Wardrobe*. Aslan did all the work—Edmund's only job would be to ask forgiveness and accept Aslan's gift of dying for him. Okay, so God makes it possible for all people—all who have sinned—to live with him. It's a great gift; but to have any benefit from it, don't you have to open it?

If a UPS package arrives at your front door but you don't open it, you will never experience the pleasure that the gift inside might have given you. If you let the Christmas gifts with your name on them stay under the tree (bet you've never done that!), you won't be able to enjoy those gifts, will you?

So what's your part in all of this? How do you receive God's gift to you?

4. If you confess with your mouth that Jesus is Lord and believe in your heart that God raised him from the dead, you will be saved. For it is by believing in

your heart that you are made right with God, and it is by confessing with your mouth that you are saved (Romans 10:9-10).

> **Confess with your mouth.** *Confess* is a little word that leads to big results. To confess something means to admit it. To confess that Jesus is Lord is to admit that he is God and that you want him (not your sins) to be the Lord—the Ruler—of your life, now and forever.
>
> What do you need to believe? That Jesus, the Son of God, died and came back to life. In other words, Easter is not just a holiday when the Easter bunny brings eggs for everyone. (You can read about the first Easter—Resurrection Sunday—in John 20.)
>
> But believing isn't just agreeing that something is true. After all, even Satan and the demons know that Jesus died and came back to life. In the Bible, the word *belief* involves *trust*. It is a belief that leads to a choice. We choose to depend on Jesus and follow him, seeking to do what he tells us to do.
>
> **Believe in your heart.** If you believe with all your heart that Jesus really died for you and rose again, you'll be "made right with God." Remember point 1 of this guide to getting to Heaven (on page 180)? When you trust in Jesus, you no longer fall short of the standard God expects. God doesn't see your sins anymore. He just sees his perfect Son, Jesus, in

front of you. God knows you are following Jesus, and someday he will have a home ready for you in Heaven.

Jesus said to his disciples, "Rejoice that your names are written in heaven" (Luke 10:20, NIV). That's a reference to being in the Lamb's Book of Life. Can you think of anything that could give us greater joy than that?

Jesus also said, "There will be more rejoicing in heaven over one sinner who repents than over ninety-nine righteous persons who do not need to repent" (Luke 15:7, NIV). Repenting involves saying we were wrong and that we're sorry, and asking God's forgiveness. Jesus is saying that whenever someone repents and turns to God, there's a party in Heaven with a lot of celebrating!

Have those in Heaven been able to celebrate yet because you've repented of your sin and trusted Christ to save you? Or are they still waiting for you to do that? You can admit right now that you've done wrong things and ask God to forgive you.

Remember, we were all made for a person and a place. Jesus is the person. Heaven is the place. You don't have to wonder whether you're going to Heaven. *You can know that today.* (If you have questions or doubts about this, talk to a parent or grandparent, a Christian neighbor, or somebody from your church who knows Jesus. They will be glad to help.)

THE GREAT STORY THAT GOES ON FOREVER

God raised us up with Christ and seated us with him in the heavenly realms in Christ Jesus, in order that in the coming ages he might show the incomparable riches of his grace.

EPHESIANS 2:6-7, NIV

*In the Great Hall of Cair Paravel . . . in the presence of all their
friends and to the sound of trumpets, Aslan solemnly crowned
them and led them to the four thrones amid deafening shouts of,
"Long Live King Peter! Long Live Queen Susan! Long Live
King Edmund! Long Live Queen Lucy!"
"Once a king or queen in Narnia, always a king or queen. Bear it
well, Sons of Adam! Bear it well, Daughters of Eve!" said Aslan. . . .
So the children sat on their thrones, and sceptres were put into their
hands and they gave rewards and honours to all their friends. . . .
And that night there was a great feast in Cair Paravel.*

C. S. Lewis, *The Lion, the Witch and the Wardrobe*

When five-year-old Emily Kimball was in the hospital and heard she was going to die, she started to cry. Even though she loved Jesus and wanted to be with him in Heaven, she didn't want to leave her family behind.

But Emily's mother had a fantastic idea. She asked Emily to step through a doorway into another room, then closed the door behind her. One at a time, Emily's entire family came through the door to join her in that room.

Her mother explained that this was how it would be when Emily died. It made sense to her. Emily would be the first to go through death's door. Eventually, the rest of the family would follow, each joining her on the other side. There they would all be together again after being apart for a little while.

The new picture in Emily's mind was a great encouragement to her. (I'm looking forward to meeting Emily when I get to Heaven. You may want to look her up too! Maybe we can all have a party together.)

The picture would have been even more complete if someone representing Jesus had been in the room to greet Emily as she entered—along with angels and Bible characters and loved ones who had already died. Also, it would have helped if the room had been beautiful, with lots of exciting things to do. And even better if it had also contained pictures of a huge, unexplored New Earth, where Emily and her family and friends would one day go to live with Jesus forever. Because . . . if we know him, that's *exactly* what the Bible promises we have to look forward to!

My wife, Nanci, and I have spent some wonderful moments with our family and friends—at Christmas, on vacation, in restaurants, at sporting events, and simply in the family room after dinner. Sometimes it's been so good that we've said, "It just doesn't get any better than this." Have you ever had a great moment when you felt that way?

Well, guess what? It *does* get better than this.
And that's actually good news! Because no matter how good the very best moments of this life
have been for us, it's just a tiny sample of what's
to come. The most ordinary moment in Heaven
will be much better than the most special moment
here! And we'll never worry that things are about
to take a turn for the worse. Because they never
will!

Living Now in Light of Heaven

I hope that you are excited about going to Heaven.
And I hope you'll think about it every day. Remember, the Bible says to "set your hearts" and "set your
minds on things above" (Colossians 3:1-2, NIV).

If we think of what God tells us about Heaven,
we won't fall for Satan's lies about it.

Listen to what Peter, one of Jesus' disciples,
said about how we should live because we know
we're going to Heaven:

What holy and godly lives you should live,
looking forward to the day of God and hurry-
ing it along. . . . We are looking forward to

the new heavens and new earth he has promised, a world filled with God's righteousness.

And so, dear friends, while you are waiting for these things to happen, make every effort to be found living peaceful lives that are pure and blameless in his sight.

And remember, the Lord's patience gives people time to be saved. (2 Peter 3:11-15)

If we understand what "the new heavens and new earth" really means, we will certainly look forward to it. (And if we're not looking forward to it, that must mean we don't understand it.)

But notice Peter's emphasis on "what holy and godly lives" we should be living! He says that while we wait for our eternal future with God, we should "make every effort" to live a "pure and blameless" life.

Now is our opportunity to live for Jesus in a world where most people don't believe in him. By obeying God's Word and not giving in to pressure to do wrong things, we please Jesus and prepare ourselves to live forever in Heaven.

Looking forward to Heaven makes hard decisions easier. It helps us to resist temptation. Moses stayed faithful to God because "he was looking ahead to his great reward" (Hebrews 11:26).

Ask yourself if you really believe you're going to live forever in a place where Christ is the center of everything and the source of all joy. Do you believe that God is using even the hard times in your life to prepare you to be one of his rulers on the New Earth? Do you really look forward to a New Earth "filled with God's righteousness"?

If you do—and I sure hope you do—then you will want to get a head start on Heaven by living for Jesus right *now*.

And don't forget Peter's other reason why Christ is waiting to bring his kingdom to Earth forever. He wants to allow time for "everyone to repent" (2 Peter 3:9). If you already know Jesus, then look around you and ask who you can pray for and share Jesus with while there is still time.

Farewell to the Shadowlands

In the final book of the Narnia series, *The Last Battle*, C. S. Lewis paints a beautiful picture of

the eternal Heaven. Early in the book, Jill and
Eustace are traveling on a train when suddenly
they find themselves in Narnia. When their adventure appears to be over, the children are seeing lots
of beautiful things and enjoying many good friends.
They don't want to leave the wonders of Narnia—
especially Aslan. They're afraid they'll be sent back
to Earth again.

Then the Lion gives the children some good
news:

"There *was* a real railway accident," said Aslan
softly. "Your father and mother and all of you
are—as you used to call it in the Shadowlands—
dead. The term is over: the holidays have begun.
The dream is ended: this is the morning."

Lewis concludes the entire Chronicles of
Narnia with one of my favorite paragraphs ever:

And as He spoke He no longer looked to them
like a lion; but the things that began to happen after that were so great and beautiful that
I cannot write them. And for us this is the
end of all the stories, and we can most truly

say that they all lived happily ever after. But for them it was only the beginning of the real story. All their life in this world and all their adventures in Narnia had only been the cover and the title page: now at last they were beginning Chapter One of the Great Story which no one on earth has read: which goes on forever: in which every chapter is better than the one before.

Doesn't that sound awesome? Well, even though the story is fiction, these words speak of something that is absolutely true. After reading this book (the one in your hands), and hearing what the Bible says about God and Heaven, I hope you are really excited about your home in Heaven.

If you know Jesus, I look forward to meeting you someday, because we will be together in Heaven. And after that, we'll walk on the New Earth, side by side. We'll smile and laugh and tell the greatest stories and have new adventures. Every chapter of our lives *will* be better than the one before!

On the New Earth, with the Lord we love and our family and friends who love him too, we'll begin the greatest of all adventures. We'll live in a glorious new universe that's waiting for us to rule and explore it under the leadership of Jesus. *He* will be the center of all things, the source of all joy. Because of who our God is and how much he loves us, *his joy will be our joy*. And therefore our joy will never end.

And right when we think to ourselves, *It just doesn't get any better than this*—it will!

• • •

"They say Aslan is on the move—perhaps has already landed."

And now a very curious thing happened. None of the children knew who Aslan was any more than you do; but the moment the Beaver had spoken these words everyone felt quite different. Perhaps it has sometimes happened to you in a dream that someone says something which you don't understand but in the dream it feels as if it had some enormous meaning— either a terrifying one which turns the whole dream into a nightmare or else a lovely meaning too lovely to put into words, which makes the dream so beautiful that you remember it

all your life and are always wishing you could
get into that dream again. It was like that now.
At the name of Aslan each one of the children
felt something jump in its inside. Edmund felt
a sensation of mysterious horror. Peter felt suddenly brave and adventurous. Susan felt as if
some delicious smell or some delightful strain
of music had just floated by her. And Lucy got
the feeling you have when you wake up in the
morning and realize that it is the beginning of
the holidays or the beginning of summer.

C. S. Lewis, *The Lion, the Witch and the Wardrobe*

About the Author

RANDY ALCORN is an author and the founder and director of Eternal Perspective Ministries (EPM), a nonprofit ministry dedicated to teaching principles of God's Word and assisting the church in ministering to the unreached, unfed, unborn, uneducated, unreconciled, and unsupported people around the world. His ministry focus is communicating the strategic importance of using our earthly time, money, possessions and opportunities to invest in need-meeting ministries that count for eternity. He accomplishes this by analyzing, teaching, and applying the biblical truth.

Before starting EPM in 1990, Randy served as a pastor for fourteen years. He has a Bachelor of Theology and Master of Arts in Biblical Studies from Multnomah University and an Honorary Doctorate from Western Seminary in Portland, Oregon and has taught on the adjunct faculties of both.

A *New York Times* bestselling author of over 50 books, including Heaven (over one million sold), *The Treasure Principle* (over two million sold), *If God Is Good*, *Happiness*, and the award-winning novel *Safely Home*. His books sold exceed eleven million copies and have been translated into over seventy languages. Randy has written for many magazines including EPM's issues-oriented

Eternal Perspectives as well as articles for The Gospel Coalition and Desiring God Ministries. He is active daily on Facebook and Twitter, has been a guest on more than 700 radio, television and online programs including Focus on the Family, FamilyLife Today, and Revive Our Hearts.

Randy resides in Gresham, Oregon, with his wife, Nanci. They have two married daughters and five grandsons. Randy enjoys hanging out with his family, biking, underwater photography, research, listening to audiobooks and reading.

Contact Eternal Perspective Ministries at epm.org or 39085 Pioneer Blvd., Suite 206, Sandy, OR 97055 or 503.668.5200. Follow Randy on Facebook: facebook .com/randyalcorn, Twitter: twitter.com/randyalcorn, and on his blog: epm.org/blog.

For parents and older kids: If you want to learn a lot more about Heaven and the New Earth and the exciting things God has in store for us, see Randy Alcorn's 476-page book *Heaven* from Tyndale House Publishers. For shorter reflections on the world to come, see Randy's *50 Days of Heaven,* also from Tyndale House.

MORE GREAT
ONE YEAR PRODUCTS
FOR YOUR FAMILY!

 The One Year® Devotions for Kids

 The One Year® Devotions for Girls Starring Women of the Bible

 The One Year® Devos for Girls

 The One Year® Devos for Animal Lovers

 The One Year® Devotions for Boys

 The One Year® Devotions for Boys 2

Available wherever books are sold

TYNDALE

www.tyndale.com/kids

CP0014

BEGIN YOUR JOURNEY TO THE GOOD LIFE NOW!

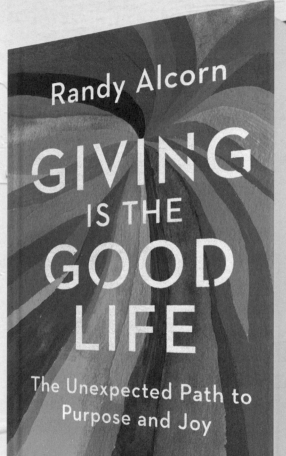

In *Giving Is the Good Life*, Randy Alcorn invites you to discover a bigger view of God and helps you see and joyfully embrace what the *good life* is really all about.

CP1528

Compassion Products from Tyndale House Publishers

Friends Around the World Activity Book

This activity book includes recipes, puzzles, crafts, and games that introduce kids to the joys and struggles of friends from far away. As they interact with the activities in the book and learn about life in other countries, kids will connect with and develop a heart of compassion for people around the world.

Who is Compassion?

The Philippines: An Interactive Family Experience

+ **Established in 1952, Compassion is an international organization whose mission is to release children from poverty in Jesus' name.**

+ **All Compassion-sponsored children have the opportunity to develop their God-given potential and to be released from spiritual, economic, social, and physical poverty.**

+ **Three things make Compassion distinct. Their ministry is:**

1. **Christ-centered**
2. **Child-focused**
3. **Church-based**

+ **Compassion has 1.2 million child sponsors reaching children in 25 countries.**

Walk through the everyday life of kids and young adults living in poverty in the Philippines as they share their hopes, dreams, and joys. Vibrant illustrations and panoramic videos bring you into the Philippines, and the crafts, recipes, prayers, and devotions build kinship with families across the ocean. See the world through God's eyes—no passport required.

Friends Around the World Atlas

Colorfully illustrated maps and interesting facts introduce children to 25 countries where Compassion International is releasing babies, children, and young adults from poverty in Jesus' name.

Releasing children from poverty
Compassion
in Jesus' name

Tyndale House Publishers, Inc.
Carol Stream, IL

A Compassion International® resource published by Tyndale House Publishers, Inc.

CP1502

Want to know more?
READ RANDY ALCORN'S *HEAVEN*.

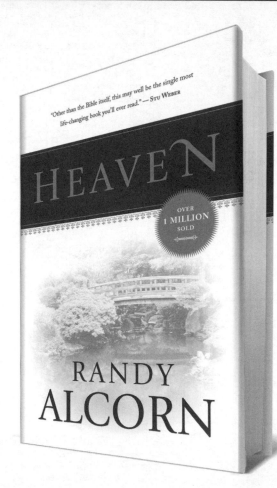

AVAILABLE ONLINE AND WHEREVER BOOKS ARE SOLD. CP0509